THE WALL STREET
SELF-DEFENSE MANUAL

OTHER SLATE TITLES FROM ATLAS BOOKS

Backstabbers, Crazed Geniuses, and Animals We Hate:
The Writers of Slate's "Assessment" Column Tell It Like It Is

The Best of Slate: A 10th Anniversary Anthology

THE WALL STREET SELF-DEFENSE MANUAL

A CONSUMER'S GUIDE TO INTELLIGENT INVESTING

HENRY BLODGET

 ATLAS BOOKS

New York

Atlas Books, LLC
10 E. 53rd St., 35th Fl.
New York NY 10022
www.atlasbooks.net

Library of Congress Cataloging-in-Publication Data
Blodget, Henry
   The Wall Street self-defense manual : a consumer's guide to intelligent investing / by Henry Blodget.—1st ed.
      p. cm.
   Includes bibliographical references and index.
   ISBN-10: 0-9777433-2-2 (alk. paper)
   ISBN-13: 978-0-9777433-2-2
   1. Investments—United States. 2. Investment analysis—United States. I. Title.

HG4910.B578 2006
332.6—dc22

                                        2006024993

Contents

PART 3 **A SOLUTION** **225**

Note to Reader

This book contains opinions about investing and Wall Street, as well as generic advice about how to improve long-term returns. Every investor's situation is different and the advice is not tailored for any particular reader.

Due to the nature of the subject matter, my publisher and I cannot guarantee the wisdom of any words in this book, and we caution that they may not, in fact, be worth the paper they are printed on (approximately one dollar per copy). I have tried to draw helpful lessons from the past, but the future has a nasty habit of being different from the past, and I do not have a crystal ball. My publisher and I hope this book helps you invest more intelligently, but we are not responsible for any losses (or foregone gains) if it doesn't.

This book grew out of a series of articles I wrote for *Slate*, as well as columns in *Fortune*, *Business 2.0*, *Euromoney* and *Newsweek International*. I have posted links to some of these articles, and further reading, on www.wallstreetself defense.com.

Introduction

This book won't tell you how to pick stocks. It won't tell you how to get rich quick. It won't tell you how to whip Warren Buffett in your spare time.

What this book will tell you is how to be a smarter investor. It will tell you what matters to intelligent investing and what doesn't (97% of what you hear). It will tell you why you shouldn't *try* to pick stocks, get rich quick or whip Warren Buffett. It will tell you how to evaluate Wall Street products and services. It will tell you how to avoid crippling mistakes. It will tell you how to earn a better return than—if not the Oracle of Omaha—most professional investors, without even sacrificing your *spare* time.

Let me begin, however, by acknowledging an obvious irony: My writing this book. Because, yes, I am *that* Henry Blodget. . .

Well, let's start at the beginning.

I grew up around Wall Street. My first visit to the New York Stock Exchange came at fifteen, a wide-eyed tour through trading booths, storms of paper, and runners darting up and down aisles. My father was a banker, but my mother was the market guru in the family: If my dad had only bought Xerox, she observed, we wouldn't have had money problems. My father, meanwhile, was as concerned about the market's ability to destroy fortunes as to create them. The Wall Street story I heard most often growing up was about how my mother's once-rich grandfather had lost everything while riding the Trans-Siberian Railway during the Great Crash of 1929.*

My Wall Street career began in 1994, in the corporate finance training program at Prudential Securities. My experiences over the next decade, which included the orgiastic peak of an eighteen-year bull market, a brutal crash, and my ignominious departure from the industry, have, by now, been chronicled ad nauseam (although, unfortunately, for legal reasons, not yet by me). Here's a quick summary:

In August 1995, the explosive market debut of a company called Netscape sparked an Internet gold rush. The new industry created a need for new specialists, and, in 1996, after two years in Prudential's technology group, I was plucked away by Oppenheimer & Co. to fill an Internet research chair. Brokerage analysts are ranked against competitors at other firms, and in my first year, I finished dead last. I learned quickly, though, and soon moved up, winning accolades from clients, the *Wall Street Journal, Institutional Investor,* Greenwich Associates and others.

For obvious reasons, bull markets lure millions of people into the stock trading game. Until late 1998, I was only peripherally aware that the stock market had gone mainstream (as I'll describe, analysts mainly serve professional investors, not individuals), but one morning I learned firsthand. I boosted my price target on Amazon, a controversial $240 stock, to $400 a share ($67 in today's split**). This is no different than taking a target on a $24 stock to $40, but the extra

---

*The reality was more complex, but I carried the image with me: My great-grandfather getting on the train a millionaire and getting off a pauper.

zero hit a media and zeitgeist nerve. The call reverberated around the electronic world, and two weeks later, when Amazon temporarily blasted through $400, I found myself in the odd position of being a financial celebrity.

In early 1999, I moved to Merrill Lynch, where I led the global Internet research team for three years. I was mostly right about the stocks I followed, and I soon became the top-ranked analyst in the industry. For a frantic two years, I was all over the globe—and, thanks to the brief and unfortunate popularity of do-it-yourself stock picking—all over newspapers, radio, and TV. By the spring of 2000, among professional investors, I was the "most read" analyst on Wall Street—and I had become a familiar name on Main Street, as well. Unfortunately, despite believing that the early Internet boom was probably a bubble—and often saying so—I waited too long to pull the plug, and, for much of that year, I was disastrously wrong.

If missing the top had been my only mistake, I would have survived (in part because almost everyone else missed it, too). I also made a more serious mistake, however, which was to write a lot of emotional, unprofessional e-mails, especially during the heat of the crash. Later, amid the wreckage, when the press, public, and regulators began calling for blood, my e-mails did me in. In the 1990s, research analysts had played a significant role in investment banking transactions, and after an investigation of this practice, I was accused by New York State Attorney General Eliot Spitzer of having made remarks in e-mails that were "inconsistent" with my research (popular

---

**When a company "splits" its stock, it increases the number of shares without changing the total value of the company. As a result, in a 2-for-1 stock split, the price of each share usually gets cut in half. Since December 1998, Amazon has split its stock 2-for-1 and 3-for-1. Thus, my $400 target is the equivalent of $67 in today's shares.

translation: "privately trashing stocks he was publicly recommending"). Along with others, I agreed to pay a humongous fine and be barred from the industry.

To say this was devastating would be an understatement. I loved the business and my colleagues, and, ironically, I had prided myself on handling the conflicts better than many analysts. To not only get benched, therefore, but to have my reputation shattered, was gut-wrenching. Wall Street has an aphorism for disasters in which every constructive option has been explored and there is nothing left to say: "It is what it is." It was what it was, and eventually I realized I had no choice but to figure out what to do despite it.

Which brings us back to this book. One benefit of getting tossed out of your industry is that you get to look at it from the outside. (And I should say here that by "industry," I don't just mean the brokerage business. I mean the whole brokerage industrial complex—brokerage firms, mutual funds, investment advisors, the investment media and the dozens of other businesses that operate in and around the markets.) This perspective helped me see that there is still a vast gulf between how most outsiders think the business works and how it really works—a gulf that frustrates not only outsiders but insiders. It helped me discover that many investment practices I thought were worthwhile, were actually a waste of money and time. And it helped me understand how, in a variety of ways, often with good intentions, Wall Street helps many small investors screw themselves.

The Big Secret (Shhh. . .)

The secret to intelligent investing is not news. It won't fill you with excitement or make you feel like a market wizard. It won't make you rich quick or solve your money problems. It won't relieve you of the need to do what most Americans hate to do (save). It won't impress your friends or make you the toast of cocktail parties. It will, however, make you a lot of money. Here it is:

Diversify your assets, reduce your costs, and *get out of the way*.

That's it. Why? Because the market odds are in your favor. In a casino, if you play long enough, you will lose. In the financial markets, if you play long enough—and don't make mistakes—you should win. Unfortunately, not making mistakes is easier said than done.

For example, if these statements don't ring true, you are probably throwing money away:

- No one knows what the market is going to do.
- The only part of your return you can control is your costs.
- Most investors who seem skillful are just lucky.
- "Long-term" investing means decades, not years.
- Investing in stocks will almost certainly not make you rich.
- Most mutual funds are a rip-off.
- Cash and bonds are risky.
- The biggest risk to your investment return is you.

One problem, much lamented, is that our interests differ from the interests of those who tell us what to do. Despite the squawks of the media, this isn't scandalous; it's just reality: There isn't a business on the planet (including the media business) in which the interests of employees, customers and owners are perfectly aligned. Another problem is that one size does not fit all: Good advice for a hedge fund might be terrible advice for you. A third problem is that, all else being equal, we would rather have fun than be bored, and investing unintelligently can be *really* fun. A fourth problem is that we are genetically programmed to make investing mistakes.

The upshot is that most of us throw away thousands of dollars a year on bad advice, shoddy or overpriced investment products and poor choices—and far more over our lifetimes on subpar returns. If investing were only a diversion—like stamp collecting, say—this wouldn't matter. Thanks to troubled Medicare and Social Security systems and a shift away from traditional pensions, however, intelligent investing has become critical to our future independence and self-esteem.

We invest unintelligently, in part, because we lack a framework with which to evaluate the bombardment of advice emanating from Wall Street, the media, advisors and friends. The first part of this book, A Self-Defense Framework, provides one. The second part of the book, Practicing Self-Defense, applies the framework to financial advisors, mutual funds, hedge funds, investment research, and the investment media, and shows why, despite Wall Street's dangers, *you* will always be the biggest risk to your returns. The third part, A Solution, describes an investment plan that allows you to make mistakes but still generate an above average long-term return.

Investment books usually come in two flavors: the you-too-can-be-Warren-Buffett type, which promises to tell you how to get as rich as Croesus, and the what-they-don't-want-you-to-know type, which portrays Wall Street as a conspiracy of shysters. This book is neither. The average investor will *not* get tremendously rich in the stock market, and Wall Street is actually not out to screw you.

We love to dream, and we never tire of scandal, so these two genres will always be with us. Unfortunately, neither will tell you what you most need to know to make smarter decisions and get Wall Street working for rather than against you. For that, there's *The Wall Street Self-Defense Manual*.

PART I
A SELF-DEFENSE FRAMEWORK

How to Get Rich

First things first. I have been advised that if I don't promise to tell you how to get rich in the markets, you won't read this book. So let me get that out of the way.

> How to Get Rich: Invest $100,000 in a *low-cost* equity index fund for fifty years. This should make you about $11 million.*

Yes, it's no get-rich-*quick* scheme, and there is fine print: This performance is not guaranteed. You must reinvest all dividends. You must make the investment in a tax-free account. Inflation will maul you. But no investment strategy is more likely to make you rich than the combination of significant savings, equity returns and time.

I have also been advised to tell you how Wall Street will take you to the cleaners. So let me get that out of the way, too.

> How to Get Taken To the Cleaners: Invest $100,000 in an *average-cost* equity mutual fund for fifty years. This should make you about $6 million . . . and *cost* you about $5 million.**

That's right. Thanks to the magic of compounding, $100,000 invested in a low-cost fund for half a century should grow to $11 million. Thanks to the black magic of advisory

---

*A "low-cost equity index fund" charges about 0.1%–0.2% of invested assets per year.

**An "average-cost equity mutual fund" charges about 1.5% of invested assets per year.

fees, meanwhile, $100,000 in an average-cost fund should grow to $6 million. That average-cost fund, in other words, will probably cost you $5 million over fifty years.

Wait—where will that $5 million go, again? Will you get swindled? No, assuming you choose your own fund, you will just be making a poor choice. The primary source of a mutual fund's return is the *market*, not the fund, and the average fund subtracts more value than it adds. Every dollar you pay in fund fees, moreover, is a dollar that will no longer compound in your account, and over the long run this lost compounding will cost you far more than the fees (in this example, $4 million vs. $1 million). In other words, you will take yourself to the cleaners—with Wall Street's help.

Here are two more ways to get rich: 1) save more, 2) work in the asset-management business. If you do the latter, you can make a pile of money even if your returns are poor. And here are two more ways to get taken to the cleaners: 1) trade too much, 2) shove your money under a mattress. Frequent trading will likely cost you several percentage points of return per year. After fifty years of average inflation, meanwhile, every dollar you have now will be worth less than a quarter.

Again, the key to investing intelligently is avoiding mistakes and letting the markets do the work. The mistake you make by buying an average-cost mutual fund is that "average-cost" is actually mind-bogglingly expensive. The mistake you make by shoving your money under a mattress is that currency is usually a terrible investment. The mistake you make if you trade frequently is that, in most cases, you would do better if you just bought and held. This last mistake, by the way, doesn't only hurt day traders. It hurts almost all of us. The first step toward avoiding it is to draw a distinction between investing and entertainment.

The Greatest Show on Earth

What is as challenging as chess and as thrilling as poker? What is played twenty-four hours a day, seven days a week? What is so difficult that only a fraction of professionals do it well but so deceptively simple that even dabblers feel skilled? What offers the celebrity glitz of Hollywood, the dynastic wealth of dictators and kings and the soap opera plots of daytime television? What is legal and encouraged in fifty states but resembles an activity banned in forty-nine? What other than sex, love and death provides grist for so many storytelling mills?

The greatest show on earth, that's what. The financial markets are fascinating, entertaining and fun. In fact, for certain personality types, they are more fascinating, entertaining and fun than most forms of actual "entertainment," many of which are seen as perfectly legitimate ways to spend hard earned money and time.*

What's more, the financial markets can make you money. The odds on Wall Street are (usually) better than the odds in Las Vegas, and even reasonable people can't get enough of

*For other personality types, of course, the financial markets are bewildering, frightening or a colossal bore—all of which create their own risks.

Vegas. You can play the markets without leaving home, from New York or the North Pole. You can play anytime. In the financial markets, there's always something to watch, think and talk about.

But now hear this: If you're serious about investing intelligently, you need to draw a distinction between investing for your future (hereafter: investing) and investing for fun, challenge and entertainment (hereafter: speculating). We will return to this distinction, but for now, let's define "speculating" as any move not made as part of a carefully developed investment plan or any move designed to pay off in less than five years.

There's nothing inherently wrong with speculating: If golf, poker, rock-climbing, and other expensive and/or risky pastimes are okay, then so is speculating. Speculators provide liquidity to markets and fund the development of industries, both of which are positive. But many speculators mistake themselves for investors, so you should be aware of what you are doing. You should know that the long-term return on your speculating will likely be lower than the long-term return on your investing, probably much lower. You should know that the difference between the two returns is entertainment cost and that this cost will likely amount to more than, say, dinner and a movie. You should know, in fact, that this cost could mean the difference between a comfortable retirement and an uncomfortable one.

Easy, you say? You just won't speculate? Well, here's the bad news: Compared to speculating, investing is *boring*. Once you get the basics right, you won't have much to watch, do or talk about. You won't be able to endlessly compare your performance to Warren Buffett's. You won't be able to brag about your brilliant picks. You won't be a font of opinions and prophecies. You won't be able to justify watching CNBC all day, gabbing with your broker, or obsessively checking Yahoo! Finance. In fact, to paraphrase oven designer Ron Popeil, you won't be able to do much more than set it and forget it.

Investing, furthermore—at least investing *well*—will mean ignoring almost everything you see and hear about the markets. It will mean tuning out friends, neighbors, co-workers, gurus and advisors who are alternately panicking or making money hand over fist (and urging you to do the same). It will mean committing to a strategy and sticking with it for *decades*. It will mean saying no to almost everything that seems exciting, challenging and interesting about the markets, including the chance to get rich quick. It will mean playing a different investing game than almost everyone you know, and continuing to play it even when doing so seems stupid, scary and wrong.

Investing intelligently, in other words, will be *hard*. Not because it's technically difficult—it isn't—but because the most powerful force in the markets is human nature, and we're all human. No matter how much you learn, you will always be led astray by boredom, distraction, peer pressure, overconfidence, inertia, envy, fear and greed.

But don't worry. Investing intelligently does not mean that you will have to abandon speculating forever. In fact, there is a simple way to have your cake and eat (a slice of) it, too, and still do better than the majority of investors. I'll describe this strategy in detail at the end of the book. For now, as a first lesson in Wall Street self-defense, just know that most of what passes for "investing" is really just an expensive parlor game, one that costs most players a lot of money, one that you don't have to play.

Why Bother?

If investing intelligently isn't going to be fun or make you rich quick, then why do it? In short, because if you don't, you'll be screwed. Traditional pension plans are disappearing, health care costs are skyrocketing, and Social Security payments, if they actually materialize, will barely fund trailer park retirements. By the time you retire, you will need to plug the gap between Social Security, et al, and the kind of life you want to live. How much will you need to do that? More than you think.

Studies suggest that, if you retire at 65, you should spend only 4% of your nest egg per year to be confident it will last the rest of your life (5% if you want to roll the longevity dice). If you retire tomorrow, therefore, every $100,000 of savings would allow you to spend $4,000 per year—assuming you don't have to pay taxes on the withdrawals, as you would with most IRAs, annuities and long-term stock holdings, and, importantly, assuming that you aren't paying steep advisory fees on your nest egg. If you have to pay either taxes or fees, your "safe" withdrawals will be considerably less.

Assume $100,000 of after-tax savings for each $4,000 of spending, and here's your required retirement fund:

Retirement Date: Today
Withdrawal Rate: 4%

Amount Necessary to Fund the Following
Spending for 30 Years:

Annual Spending	Required Nest Egg
$25,000	$625,000
$50,000	$1,250,000
$75,000	$1,875,000
$100,000	$2,500,000
$125,000	$3,125,000
$150,000	$3,750,000
$175,000	$4,375,000
$200,000	$5,000,000

And that's if you retire tomorrow. If you retire a couple of decades from now, you're going to need a lot more. Why? Because at only a 3% inflation rate—less than the historical average—your money will lose a third of its value in fourteen years, half in twenty-three, and three-quarters in forty-five. If you are a forty-year-old who stuffs your cash under a mattress, by the time you retire, every dollar you have now will likely be worth less than fifty cents. To calculate your required nest egg for a retirement beginning twenty-five years from now, therefore, double the numbers above.

These depressing observations reveal the two primary goals of any intelligent investor. Namely:

1. Avoid *losing* the purchasing power of your savings (harder than it sounds, especially after tax). And, preferably,

2. *Increase* the purchasing power of your savings, after deducting the costs of investment management and advisory services, transactions, taxes and mistakes.

It would be nice if a reasonable investment goal were to "get rich," but, unfortunately, unless you plan on saving a truckload of money, this will take a long, long time. You can, of course, increase your odds of getting rich by taking a lot of risk, but this will also increase your odds of losing everything. It's a free country, and if you can leap from airplanes, smoke cigarettes and bungee jump, you can roll the market dice. But if you do and then regret it, don't waste time trying to find someone else to blame.

A Short History of Market History

Why do so many investors end up disappointed? Some fall victim to bad decisions and bad advice. Most, however, just expect too much to begin with. So here are two questions you should know the answer to:

1. How rich can you get?
2. How long will it take?

In an age that worships instant gratification, these answers, too, are depressing. Before we get to them, however, we should answer another question: How much can you *lose*? The answer to that one, sadly, is "Everything." You can't get returns without taking risks. (And the risks are actual risks, not just fine print.) The good news is, as long as you invest intelligently, your risk of losing everything is tiny. Also, as discussed, you can't avoid risk by not investing, because if you don't invest, you're practically *guaranteed* to lose: Inflation has wiped out more wealth over the centuries than any market crash.

So, how rich can you get, and how long will it take? Let's start with a short history of market history.

Stocks, it is often said, are the "best investment for the long haul." Assuming you have the correct definition of "long haul," this is true: Over the past 200 years, U.S. stocks have returned about 10% a year (7% after adjusting for inflation, which is called the *real* return), more than any other major asset class. As is illustrated below, this long-term stock return compares to long-term returns of 5.5% for U.S. Treasury bonds (2.4% real) and 3.7% for Treasury bills (a proxy for cash, which has generated a modest 0.6% real return).

Long-Term Total Returns, 1925–2005*

Asset Class	Nominal Return	Real Return
Large U.S. Stocks	10.4%	7.4%
U.S. Treasury Bonds	5.5%	2.5%
U.S. Treasury Bills	3.7%	0.6%

Believe it or not, a 7% real return can create serious wealth. Of course, don't for a minute take this to mean that stocks *always* provide the best return or even that they always provide *any* return. In fact, because the idea that "stocks are the best investment for the long haul" has become so central to the worldview of many investors, it's worth exploring what it really means. To do so, we need only review the performance of U.S. stocks in the twentieth century, a period in which total returns averaged the familiar 10%.

The century got off to a good start. In 1906, the S&P Composite, then dominated by railroad and bank stocks, hit an all-time peak of 10, after a decade-long bull market in which it had nearly tripled. That year, however, the market started going down, and, once it did, it didn't really stop going down

*Source: Ibbotson Associates, Inc.

until fifteen years later, after the Great War, by which time it had lost a third of its value.

In 1921, just as demoralized investors had all but given up, the great bull market began. Over the next eight years, stock prices exploded, with the S&P quintupling to 31 by the end of September 1929. By then, after a decade that had seen the widespread adoption of cars, phones, radios, electric appliances, lights, skyscrapers and planes, the future seemed so bright that an esteemed economist, Irving Fisher (the furthest thing from a greater fool) concluded that stocks had reached a "permanently high plateau." They hadn't. Fourteen days later came Black Monday, which kicked off the Great Crash. And three years after that, in the summer of 1932, the market bottomed at 5, down some 80% from its high. The 1932 low was lower than the 1921 low. It was, in fact, the lowest low since 1898, thirty-four years earlier. In that dark hour, as in 1921, few folks presumably considered stocks the best investment for the long haul.

The Great Crash, it is said, taught an entire generation to avoid the stock market—and no wonder. It took 1929 investors twenty-five years to get back to even in nominal terms (excluding dividends), and *twenty-nine* years after inflation. Even including dividends, U.S. stock investors were in the red for fifteen years. Of course, gradually, painfully, the Great Crash also set the stage for one of the longest bull markets in history. After a decade of volatility during the Great Depression and prelude to World War II, stocks finally resumed a steady upward course, and they maintained it for the next thirty years. In 1973, after the "go-go" Sixties and "Nifty Fifty" era in the 1970s, the S&P hit 118, more than twenty times its 1932 low and nearly four times its 1929 high. Stocks were once again, emphatically, the best investment for the long haul.

Then came the 1973–1974 bear market, which took the S&P (by then, the S&P 500), down more than 40% in two years. Stagflation, surging oil prices and soaring interest rates kept it down for another six. By the time the index finally hit a new high in 1980, stocks had treaded water for another fifteen years. From there, however, with the brief exception of the crash of 1987, the worst one-day market drop in history, it was off to the races again. By the end of the century, the S&P had again increased more than ten-fold, hitting an all-time high of 1,527 in March 2000, a run that made the great bull market of the 1920s look like a warm-up act. Of course, as it always does, boom gave way to bust, and, as of this writing, we were still well below the 2000 peak and in the middle of another long bear market again.

So stocks may be the best investment for the long haul, but the long haul is *long*. Far from notching steady appreciation of 10% a year, stocks are cyclical. In the twentieth century, complete market cycles—as defined by peak-to-peak or trough-to-trough—lasted thirty to forty years. During the bull phases, which usually lasted ten to twenty years, the market appreciated by many multiples of its trough value. During the bear phases, which lasted from three to thirty years, the market traded sideways at best.

Because analysts often base market predictions on forecasts of economic growth, it is worth noting that, in fact, the performance of the market and the economy often diverge. As Warren Buffett observed in a 2001 *Fortune* article—perhaps the wisest, pithiest snapshot of investment history ever written—the U.S. economy grew steadily in every decade of the twentieth century, even in the 1930s. Stocks, meanwhile, were far more volatile, driven by changes in earnings, interest rates, and investors' emotions. Over the long term, the stock market loosely tracks the economy, but "the long term" means decades.

Where Those Returns Come From

In addition to knowing what long-term investment returns are, it is helpful to know where they come from. Investment returns are compensation for lending or selling money. In a *debt* transaction, such as a mortgage, the capital provider rents money in exchange for interest payments. In an *equity* transaction, the capital provider sells money in exchange for an asset, such as a share of stock. As in most free-market transactions, sellers of money want to be paid as much as possible, and buyers of money want to pay as little as possible. Because capital buyers and sellers abound, competition reduces the ability of any one capital-market participant to dictate prices. Instead, prices are set by market forces—namely, risk and return and supply and demand.

Capital providers (that is, investors) don't want to sell or lend money too cheaply, lest they soon need capital themselves. They also don't want to take undue risks, such as making loans that might not be paid back or buying assets that might lose value, *without receiving adequate compensation for doing so*. Thus, rational capital providers try to evaluate, first, the risk of a specific investment opportunity, and, second, the return required to offset this risk (both easier said than done). The relationship between risk and return provides the theoretical underpinning for the long-term performance of the major asset classes. In general, less-risky investments provide lower returns, and more-risky investments provide higher ones.

There are many kinds of investment risk,* but the most basic kind is that you will lose money. The least-risky major asset class, U.S. Treasury bills, nearly guarantees that you will get your money back, so bills have paid only a negligible real rate of return (0.6% per year above inflation). The most-risky major asset class, meanwhile—stocks—come with considerable risk, at least in the short term. Stocks, therefore, have paid a significant real return (7.4% per year).** The irony, of course, is that over the long term—periods of twenty years and more—stocks have proven considerably *less risky* than bonds and bills, a fact that should comfort long-term stock investors and that might also reduce the premium that stock investors have historically received.***

Another way to understand historical stock returns is to dissect them. Shares of stock represent shares of ownership of companies—a pro rata percentage of earnings and assets. If a company increases earnings per share over time, as most healthy companies do, the theoretical value of each share (if not its price) also increases.

---

*For example, default risk, price risk, inflation risk, market risk, industry risk, company risk, liquidity risk, reinvestment risk, volatility risk, time risk and benchmark risk.

**The additional return required to compensate equity investors above that of Treasury bills is called the "equity risk premium." For several reasons, many analysts expect this premium to shrink in the future, meaning that stock returns may be closer to bond returns. The basic relationship between risk and reward, however, should remain.

***One explanation for today's high stock valuations, in fact, is that investors have clued into the idea that stocks aren't as risky as they seem, and, thus, are willing to pay more for them than they have in the past. Although this may be true, it is also nothing that a brutal, prolonged bear market won't cure (e.g., Japan from 1990–2004). The long term is long, and investors who bought stocks expecting an annual 10% return only to find that, fifteen years later, they have lost half their money, will be easily persuaded to throw in the towel.

Risk vs. Reward
One-year Returns, 1925–2005

	Average	Max/Yr	Min/Yr
Large U.S. Stocks	10%	54% / 1933	−43% / 1931
U.S. Treasury Bonds	6%	40% / 1982	−9% / 1967
U.S. Treasury Bills	4%	15% / 1981	0% / 1938

Risk vs. Reward
20-Year Returns, 1926–2005

	Average	Max/Yr	Min/Yr
Large U.S. Stocks	10%	18% / 1980–1999	3% / 1929–1948
U.S. Treasury Bonds	6%	12% / 1982–2001	−9% / 1950–1969
U.S. Treasury Bills	4%	8% / 1972–1991	0% / 1931–1950

Between 1926 and 2005, the aggregate earnings per share of all U.S. companies increased about 5% per year, driven by both inflation (3%) and real earnings growth (2%). Together, these factors contributed about half of the total 10% annual equity return. An additional 4% came from dividends, and the final 1% resulted from an increase in the price investors were willing to pay for each dollar of earnings (the price-earnings ratio).

This highlights another key difference between stocks and bonds. Stockholders participate in the benefits of economic growth. Bond-holders and cash-holders don't.

Remember: God Blessed America

Before you forecast a 7% inflation-adjusted stock return forever, it is also worth noting that the U.S. experience in the twentieth century was an exceptionally positive one. The United States

came out on the winning side of two world wars, enjoyed phenomenal economic growth and never experienced the hyperin-
flation that ravaged investors in other countries. The real return
of a sixteen-country "world index" created by London Business
School professors Elroy Dimson, Paul Marsh and Mike Staunton
in a book called *Triumph of the Optimists* was only 5%. Even this
index, moreover, may have overstated average world stock performance, as it did not include emerging markets or countries
like China and Russia, in which assets were simply seized by
revolutionaries (a quick route to a poor return).

Nor did most of the United States' 10% long-term equity
return even come from *price* appreciation, an assumption that
usually follows the observation that stocks are the best investment for the long haul. Rather, almost half of the return came
from *reinvested dividends*. According to *Triumph of the Optimists,*
4.7% of the total U.S. twentieth century stock return of 10.1%
per year was produced by dividend reinvestment.* Without
this, stocks were *not* the best investment for the long haul,
even in the United States (bonds were).

So, what "stocks are the best investment for the long haul"
means, according to Wharton professor Jeremy Siegel, who
wrote an excellent book on the subject,** is that, in every
thirty-year period since the late–1800s, stocks have outperformed bonds and cash. This is true for most twenty-year periods, too, and of five- and ten-year periods. It has even held true
in countries like Japan and Germany, whose bouts with hyper-
inflation completely *wiped out* the value of bonds and cash.

---

*The reinvestment of dividends contributes more to total return than most
investors think. By reinvesting dividends, an investor accumulates more
shares, which then appreciate in price and pay more dividends, and so on.
Over time, these compounding effects add significantly to the total return.

**Stocks for the Long Run.

Good Things for Those Who Waited

So, if you had owned U.S. stocks for the long haul, reinvested dividends, never spent a dime on transaction costs and paid no taxes, how rich would you have gotten? Very. According to Professor Siegel, who studied the 195 years from 1802 to 1997, every dollar invested in 1802 would have appreciated to $7.5 million by 1997. Wow. Of course, as breathtaking as this statistic is, it is also irrelevant. In the real world, your investing lifetime will (if you're lucky) be limited to about fifty years. You will also likely spend some of your gains, pay pots of money in costs and taxes, and get clobbered by inflation. According to Siegel, inflation alone would reduce your 195-year total to $558,945.

Siegel's point, though, is not that stocks make you rich but that stocks usually weather inflation better than bonds or cash do (because, theoretically, stocks are claims on real assets, whose value appreciates with inflation, whereas most bonds are IOUs that can be repaid in deflated currency). For example, Siegel calculates that, over the same 195-year period, the after-inflation value of $1 invested in bonds would be $803 and of $1 invested in Treasury bills $275. That's right: invest $1 in stocks and after 195 years you would have had the inflation-adjusted equivalent of $558,945. Invest it in bonds or bills, and you would have had $803 and $275, respectively. This is why stocks are said to be the best investment for the long haul.

To underscore the inflation point, it is also worth taking a peek at Siegel's calculations of the 195-year investment value of 1) a dollar invested in everyone's favorite inflation and world-crisis hedge, gold, and 2) a dollar shoved under the mattress. After 195 years, a dollar invested in gold would have been worth—drum roll, please—eighty-four cents. So much for the long-term investment value of this "precious" metal.

Then again, you would have been better off buying gold—or almost anything else—with your dollars than shoving them under the mattress. At the end of 195 years, a dollar invested in nothing was worth all of seven cents.

Value of $1 Invested from 1802–1997*
Various Asset Classes

	1802	1997
U.S. Stocks	$1	$558,945
U.S. Treasury Bonds	$1	$803
U.S. Treasury Bills	$1	$275
Gold	$1	$0.84
Nothing	$1	$0.07

Will history repeat itself? Most people assume so, but no one knows. Wise forecasters note that the past two centuries have, on balance, been extraordinarily positive for global economies and markets. In good times, history feels like a straight line of progress, up and to the right, but a broader view shows that it is often anything but. Smart investors, therefore, should never rule out the possibility that future returns could severely disappoint. At the very least, an intelligent forecaster should note that, even many years after the stock market peak, U.S. stock valuations remain high, and that, in the past, above-average valuations have preceded below-average returns. So expecting a 10% annual return from U.S. stocks seems aggressive, at least in the early part of this century.

Assuming history does repeat itself, the past is (somewhat) comforting for stock investors. It also reveals, however, that the "long run" will often feel like eternity.

*Adjusted for inflation. Source: *Stocks for the Long Run.*

How Rich You Can Get

So let's assume past is prologue and you have the fortitude and time horizon necessary to stick all of your money in stocks. Let's assume that you start with a meaningful nest egg of $100,000.* Let's further assume that you 1) invest well enough to capture the market return (easier said than done and far better than most investors do), and 2) never add or take money out. Here, after various time periods, is how rich you would get:

Initial Investment: $100,000
Annual Return: 10%

10 Years:	$259,000
20 Years:	$673,000
30 Years:	$1,745,000
40 Years:	$4,526,000
50 Years:	$11,739,000

Nearly $12 million after fifty years? Amazing! Investment advisors fall all over themselves to show you numbers like these—and no wonder. Unfortunately, the numbers are misleading.

---

*If $100,000 of savings seems like too much to even be worth contemplating, lop off a zero or two from both the initial investment and the final values. If it seems too puny to bother with, add a zero or two.

Before we discuss why, note that the vast majority of the wealth creation comes in years twenty through fifty. After twenty years—*twenty years*—you would only have $673,000. The most important determinants of your future nest egg, in other words, are the amount you save and the length of time it compounds. This reveals the real secret to getting rich in the markets: *Start investing immediately and save as much as you can.*

So, why are the numbers misleading? Because they aren't adjusted for inflation. Because they don't deduct the vast sums you will pay stockbrokers, fund managers, traders, and the tax man. Because they assume you won't make a single mistake, such as panicking in a crash and selling at the bottom. Because they assume you won't fire your advisors and prematurely generate taxes, or try to beat the market and end up lagging it. Because they assume you won't make the wise but return-reducing move of putting some of your portfolio into bonds, cash, or other volatility-reducing asset classes. Because they assume a straight-line return instead of the inevitable booms and busts. Etcetera.

Will these factors affect your returns? You bet. We'll review the agonizing details later, but here's a summary. Inflation will likely cut your purchasing power by about 3% per year. A modest cash and bond position will reduce your long-term return by 1%–2% a year. Brokers, fund managers and traders will, if you let them, help themselves to about 2% of your money each year. And Uncle Sam might swipe an additional two points of return per year.

After bonds, inflation, costs and taxes, in other words, your long-term return might drop from 10% per year to about 2%. How rich would that make you? Not very.

Initial Investment: $100,000
Annual *Real* Return after Costs and Taxes: 2%

10 Years:	$122,000
20 Years:	$149,000
30 Years:	$181,000
40 Years:	$221,000
50 Years:	$269,000

This is why it's tough to get rich in the markets. This, in part, is why even people who know better often swing for the speculative fences (which, as we will see, isn't the answer). This is why it is crucial to save as much as possible and capture as much of the market return as possible. This is why you should ignore what you can't control (market performance) and focus on what you can control (diversification and costs). The good news is, if you do the latter, you can improve your long-term return by at least three points per year. This will make a major difference in how rich you get.

To strike a more optimistic note, in fact, let's see what happens if you invest intelligently and reduce costs and taxes enough to generate a 5% real after-tax return (a return many investors will snicker at in disgust, before they generate a lower one). Remember, these numbers are adjusted for inflation, and therefore represent real increases in purchasing power.

Initial Investment: $100,000
Annual *Real* Return after Costs and Taxes: 5%

10 Years:	$163,000
20 Years:	$265,000
30 Years:	$432,000
40 Years:	$704,000
50 Years:	$1,147,000

Now that's more like it.

What if you don't have $100,000? What if you plan to save and invest over time? As long as you start immediately, you should do almost as well. If you continue saving after you have socked away $100,000, moreover, you should eventually do even better. Here, for example, is what might happen if you saved and invested $10,000 per year for the next fifteen years at a 5% real, after-tax return (i.e., the same scenario as the one above, except with a total investment of $150,000):

Initial Investment: $10,000
Annual Investments Each Year for 14 More Years: $10,000
Annual *Real* Return after Costs and Taxes: 5%

10 Years:	$142,000
20 Years:	$289,000
30 Years:	$471,000
40 Years:	$767,000
50 Years:	$1,250,000

And, finally, here's what might happen if you followed a typical savings pattern, making small contributions when you were young and salary-challenged, and bigger ones as you got older and richer.

Initial Investment: $1,000
Annual Contributions for Years 1–9: $1,000
Annual Contributions for Years 10–19: $5,000
Annual Contributions for Years 20–29: $10,000
Annual Contributions for Years 30–39: $20,000
Annual Real Return after Costs and Taxes: 5%

10 Years:	$18,000
20 Years:	$98,000
30 Years:	$295,000
40 Years:	$712,000
50 Years:	$1,159,000

That's the ticket.

So, Just Beat the Market!

Confronted with the depressing facts about real market re-turns, the natural reaction is to say, "Well, then I'll just beat the market." How will you do this? You'll buy winners and sell dogs. How will you do that? You'll find a crackerjack broker to funnel you a steady stream of "tips"—or you'll just watch CNBC, scour financial statements, and do it yourself.

And maybe you will. Half a century of performance data suggests that a handful of investors with exceptional dedica-tion, information and skill can indeed pick stocks well enough to beat the averages over the long term (many do it over the short term, but this is usually the result of luck or the vicissi-tudes of investment style, not skill). If you truly dedicate your-self to the task, therefore, you might succeed.

The same half-century of evidence, however, suggests that you almost certainly won't. Instead, like most investors, in-cluding professionals, you will probably just waste money and time. Importantly, if you do fail to beat the market over the long term, it will not be because you are incompetent or stu-pid. One dangerous misconception about investing is that the reason most investors lag the market is that they are morons. The real reason is that beating the market is *hard*. (Another dangerous misconception is that intelligent investors should

---

What "Market Efficiency" Really Means

The Efficient Market Hypothesis argues that stock prices quickly incorporate all relevant news and information and, therefore, that it is hard to beat the market by analyzing financial statements, doing industry research and performing other activities often thought to form the bedrock of sound investment decisions. Importantly, the theory does not suggest that stock prices are always right—just that they're not so wrong that investors can consistently use mispricings to generate market-beating returns.

A better way to think about market efficiency is that stock prices reflect a collective guess about how the future will unfold. Although this guess is probably wrong, it is usually less wrong than the guess of any one investor.

---

try to beat the market. On the contrary, most should begrudgingly accept the market return.)

Before continuing, we need to step back a bit, because if your friends or advisors haven't seen the light on this, they will bludgeon you with a thousand examples of funds that have "beaten the market" over such-and-such a period. They will also probably announce that *they* routinely beat the market. And in the name of Wall Street self-defense, you need to know why they are usually wrong.

Active vs. Passive Management

Most investment strategies fall into one of two camps: Those that try to beat the market (or subset of a market called an index) and those that don't. The former, called "active" strategies, employ a variety of techniques—stock picking, market timing, fund picking, sector picking—to try to beat the averages. "Passive" strategies, meanwhile, buy and hold all (or a representative sample) of the securities in an index, regardless of market conditions, with the aim of capturing the market or index return.

Importantly, passive investing does not just mean buying an S&P 500 index fund. Markets can be segmented into dozens of indices, and passive strategies can be designed to track any of them. Some of these indices, moreover, screen stocks by size, book value, earnings, price and other fundamental metrics that most investors associate with traditional stock picking techniques. Some passive investors, furthermore, apply different "weights" to different securities within the index, owning more of stocks with certain characteristics, and less of others. As passive investing has become more refined, in other words, the distinction between active and passive has become less clear-cut. At the most basic level, however, an active investor will try to "pick winners" and time the market while a passive investor will just aim to capture an index return.

Most investors are active investors. Why? Because, at first blush, active management seems by far the superior strategy. Who wouldn't want to own just winners? Who wouldn't want to dump dogs? Who wouldn't want to get out before market crashes and in before market booms? Who wouldn't want to own a fund managed by "the next Warren Buffett"? Answer? No one. As a result, most investors (or their advisors and fund managers) trade incessantly, with the aim of producing an above-market return.

Not all active investors realize that they are trying to beat the market. Some think they are just "investing." The *only*

Do Day-Traders Make Money?

In every bull market, people quit their jobs to trade full time. Should they? No. Most would do better if they just bought and held. A study of the performance of day traders on the Taiwan Stock Exchange* over a five-year period concluded that the average trader made money on a gross basis, but that, in a typical six-month period, more than 80% lost money after costs. The good news (sort of) was that *heavy* day-traders lost less money than occasional day traders, so if you're hell-bent on day-trading, you'll probably lose less if you do it full time.

reason to practice active management, however—the only reason to pick stocks, time the market, buy actively managed funds, etc.—is to try to beat the market. There was a time when advisors and fund managers could imagine that their job was to merely help clients "make sound investments," but that time is gone. The proliferation of low-cost index funds, life cycle funds and other passive vehicles has made it easy and cheap for any investor to get near-market returns. Anyone who chooses an active strategy over a passive one, therefore, is—knowingly or unknowingly—trying to beat the market.

*Professors Brad Barber, Yi-Tsung Lee, Yu-Jane Liu and Terrance Odean studied the Taiwan Stock Exchange because, for a variety of reasons, Taiwan's market is better suited for studies of day trading than the United States and other markets. The professors found that a handful of day traders did make money consistently, so if you're confident you will be a member of this elite group then, by all means, quit your job. Just don't expect your new one to be any easier.

What "Beating the Market" Means

Any intelligent discussion about beating the market has to start with a definition of what the phrase means. One popular definition is "beating the S&P 500," a broad index of large U.S. stocks. For some investors, the S&P 500 is a meaningful benchmark with which to evaluate portfolio performance. For others, however—such as those who trade small stocks—it is not. Even when the S&P 500 is the appropriate benchmark, moreover, comparing relative performance is only meaningful when one also considers relative risk.

For an investment to be worth making, it must have an expected return that compensates for its risk. A stock that offers the expected return of a Treasury bill would be a bad investment. (Just buy the safer Treasury bill.) A Treasury bond that paid real interest of 7% per year, meanwhile, would be a great investment (equity-like returns with lower risk). Thus, for an investor benchmarked against the S&P 500, the relevant question is not just "Did she beat the S&P?" but "Did she beat the S&P *while taking the same or less risk*?" Similarly, a better definition of "beating the market" is either: 1) generating a better *risk-adjusted* return than an index by picking winners, or 2) generating the index return with lower risk.

Welcome to a Zero-Sum Game

The most important thing you need to know about trying to beat the market is that, unless you possess truly superior skill, *the odds are against you*. If, like most people, you have made money in the markets, this is hard to accept. It is true, however. In aggregate, active-management returns will lag market returns, and the average active investor will lose.

Judging by the number of commentators who express surprise, dismay and/or scorn about manifestations of this sad fact—such as the observation that most professional fund managers fail to beat index funds—it is not widely understood. It is therefore worthy of a detailed explanation. There are two reasons why active management returns will always lag market (and low-cost passive) returns. First, the aggregate gross return of all investors who trade within a market must *equal* the return of the market. Second, active investors incur return-reducing costs that the market does not.*

This does not mean that the market can't be beaten. Each year, about half of the stocks in the market usually beat the market, and active managers who own more of these stocks than laggard stocks beat the market. (Whether they do this because of skill or luck is a different question, as is whether they will beat the market again next year.) What it does mean is

*Nobel Prize winner William Sharpe explains why in a short essay called "The Arithmetic of Active Management." The gross return of a passive benchmark containing every stock in a market must equal the gross return of all active funds trading the stocks in the market. If it does not, the sum of the passive returns plus the active returns would exceed the market return. Because active funds have expenses, moreover, and the passive benchmark does not, the collective return of the active funds will always be lower than that of the benchmark. The only way that active *mutual* funds can, in aggregate, beat passive benchmarks is if there is another group of traders who are much less skilled than active fund managers (for example, individual day traders). If day traders do badly enough, the mutual funds might, in aggregate, do better than the passive benchmark. On a gross basis, however, the return of all actively managed money cannot exceed that of the market as a whole.

that, taken together, the performance of *all* active managers can be no better than the market return. It also means that, after their costs are deducted, again in aggregate, active investors will do *worse* than the market return. (For a detailed example, please see the Notes.)

Before fees and costs are considered, in other words, active management is a *zero-sum game*. After fees and costs are deducted, moreover, active management is less than a zero-sum game. Specifically, it is a game in which the expected outcome is negative, in which the odds are against the average participant winning. While some active managers will win, the majority will *lose*.*

What other games have negative expected outcomes? All the games played in Las Vegas (unless you're playing for the house). Lots of people win in Las Vegas, but most people lose. If they didn't, casinos wouldn't exist. The word used to describe the playing of games in Las Vegas is *gambling*, because the odds are against you. The word used to describe active money management, meanwhile, is *investing*. This is unfortunate, because the odds are against you here, too.

Wait. Aren't the odds on Wall Street better than the odds in Las Vegas? *Some* of the odds, yes. The odds of making money by buying and holding major asset classes over several decades are excellent. The odds of doing *better than* the asset classes

---

*Strictly speaking, it is the average actively managed *dollar* that must lose, not the average active *manager*. Because a handful of investors—the top 200 institutional managers—control a large percentage of actively managed dollars, it is conceivable that a majority of *investors* could win, even though the majority of actively managed dollars lost. For this to happen, however, the top 200 institutions would have to perform worse than all other investors—a scenario that, given their awesome research and trading resources, experience and skill, seems unlikely.

through active trading, however, are negative. Most active investors end up reducing the odds (and returns) that they would have gotten from just owning the underlying assets.

Just How Bad Are Your Odds?

Your precise odds of winning the active-management game depend on your skill: better traders have better odds, worse traders have worse ones. Because so much investment performance can be the result of chance, however—and because your skill changes as you learn—you can't know in advance exactly what your odds are. What you can know is what other active investors' odds *have been in the past,* including the odds of a group of folks whose collective skill likely exceeds that of the average Joe: full-time professionals.

In the past half-century, dozens of studies have analyzed the performance of active mutual fund managers relative to passive benchmarks. Almost without exception, they have concluded that, after costs, most active managers fall short. In the most encouraging studies—encouraging for those who hold out hope that active management isn't a waste of money and time—only two-thirds of active managers lag their benchmarks. In the most discouraging, 97% do so.

Put differently, the studies suggest that the odds that an active fund will beat its passive benchmark are between 1-in-3 and 1-in-33. The latter odds, you might note, are almost the same as the odds of hitting a single number in roulette. What's worse, these odds are calculated on a *pretax* basis. Well-managed passive funds tend to be tax efficient, so, after tax, many active funds do even worse.

In roulette, moreover, if you get lucky and hit a number (1-in-38 odds), you get a "return" that comes close to compensating you for your risk (35-to-1 payout). The return doesn't *quite* compensate you for your risk, of course, because then the house wouldn't be guaranteed to win. Still, it comes close.

In the financial markets, meanwhile, if you are lucky enough to "hit the number" by beating the market or selecting a winning active fund, you will not likely be paid for your risk. Why not? Because the average active fund winner (the long shot) beats the benchmark by less than the average loser lags it. For example, a study of general equity funds by First Quadrant L.P. found that only one in five active funds beat the S&P 500 over the twenty-year period through 1998. The average winner, moreover, beat the index by 1.35% per year. The average loser, meanwhile, lagged the index by −2.64% per year. Because of these different payouts, even if investors had had a fifty-fifty shot of picking a winner, which they didn't, active funds would have been a bad bet.

Put differently, in the active-management game, investors do not get paid to accept long odds the way they do in roulette, horseracing and lotto. If they win their long-shot bets, active investors get rewarded with an expected payout that is only marginally more than they would receive for a sure thing. If they lose their long-shot bets, meanwhile, as most do, they don't just "not win"—they lose big.* Choosing active management, therefore, is, in most cases, a mistake.

---

*Here's another way to describe the active vs. passive bet (using the numbers in the First Quadrant study). I will offer you the choice of playing or not playing a game. If you choose not to play, I will pay you ten times what you would have bet if you had played. If you choose to play the game, I will ask you to pick a number between one and five, and then I will spin a five-number roulette wheel to determine which number is the "winner." If you picked the winning number, I will pay you fifteen times your bet. If you

Again, this is not to say that the odds are against active investors *making money*. In a bull market, the odds of making money are so favorable that even a basket case of an active investor can usually come out ahead (a fortuitous outcome that he or she will usually attribute to skill). The same investor will probably lose money relative to a passive strategy, however. In a bear market, the odds of making money are poor regardless of your strategy, but they are even worse when you pursue an active one.

Why isn't active management considered gambling? Three reasons, probably. First, most active investors don't realize that the odds are against them. Second, even investors who lose the active-management game sometimes make money, and, therefore, fail to see that they have lost. And, third, no self-respecting active investor believes for a minute that he will be one of the great losing majority.

pick a losing number, I will pay you only six times your bet. If you choose to play, in other words, you will have a 1-in–5 chance of winning (and taking home more than if you hadn't played) and a 4-in–5 chance of losing (and taking home a lot less). Meanwhile, I, your croupier, will keep anything you don't take home. Want to play?

Meet Your Competition

If you are like most investors, your reaction to the idea that most active investors lose will be, "So what? The odds are against success in many endeavors in life, and winners still win." If this is your attitude, you will get nothing but encouragement from Wall Street. The "you can beat the market" story is not only extremely profitable for those who make a living by facilitating active management. It is also a story you want to hear—you're a winner!—and one that plays to your ego and the American dream of independence and self-sufficiency.

Your odds of winning the active management game are lousy. But, still, you have a point. The odds are also against building a successful company, opening a successful restaurant or writing a best-selling novel—and this doesn't (and shouldn't) stop you from trying. So if, after reviewing the evidence, you really believe that you can consistently outwit most investors, then try. Better yet, go into the money management business, where you can make a fortune even if you fail. Whatever you do, don't buy the hogwash that beating the market is just a matter of reading some research, analyzing some financial statements and picking stocks or funds in your spare time.

To win the active management game, you have to consistently outsmart the vast majority of other investors. Your relative skill, therefore, matters. In this way, active management is actually different from most games in Las Vegas—craps, blackjack, roulette—in which your odds are always negative. A better analogy for active management is poker. In poker, the overall odds for the table are always negative (because the house takes a cut of every pot), but the odds for the *best* players at the table are positive. In poker, you can win if you are only average, as long as the other folks at the table stink. An intelligent poker player, therefore, need not be confident that she is world class—just that she is better than the people she is playing against.

Unfortunately, this is where the analogy ends. In the global financial markets, there are no special tables for beginners, hobbyists and suckers. There is just one table, and, every time you sit down at it, you will be competing against the best players in the world. True, you will also be competing with tens of thousands of boneheads. But the majority of your competitors will be smart, experienced, well-trained, well-informed professionals who do little but play the game.*

Is it possible for you to beat these players consistently? Yes. Is it *likely*? No.

---

*Lest the poker analogy make you think that you just have to be better than *most* investors, Dartmouth professor Kenneth French adds a further insight. If you sit down at a poker table at which you are better than five of the seven players, do you think the best two players, the ones who are better than all six of you, are happy or sad that you showed up? Happy. Your playing just means more money for them to win.

Your Competition

If you play the active management game, your competitors will be all other active investors—including many who read the same research, use the same trading tools and services, and listen to the same experts as you do. Most of these competitors will be full-time investment professionals with resources, contacts, information and experience that you can only dream of. These competitors will be working around the clock—and around the globe—seven days a week, with only one goal in mind: to *kick your ass.*

Why? Because that's the only way *they* can win. Remember that active management is a zero-sum game: Every above-market return earned by one investor must come at the expense of another. For you to beat the market, you must consistently beat most of your competitors. So it behooves you to have a good grasp of who they are.

Your competitors include thousands of professionals employed at mutual funds, hedge funds, pension funds, trusts, banks, trading desks, brokerage firms, governments, and corporations who collectively manage tens of trillions of dollars worth of money worldwide, as well as millions of small investors who manage trillions more. Do not delude yourself into thinking that, because there are more individual investors than institutional investors, you are competing against amateurs. Professional investors manage the vast majority of money and conduct the vast majority of trades. According to Charles Ellis, author of *Winning the Loser's Game,* more than 90% of the trades on the New York Stock Exchange are made by professionals. Chances are high, therefore, that the person buying from you or selling to you knows what he or she is doing.

The skill and sophistication of your competitors varies, but, on the professional side, even the average ones have enormous resources. For example, the average professional:

- researches investments for at least ten hours a day.
- has access to every news story, blog, press release, financial filing and company presentation ever published, as well as off-the-record commentary that is often far more revealing.
- spends thousands of dollars a month on primary research.
- has relationships with professional analysts at dozens of firms.
- visits dozens of companies a year.
- participates in hundreds of conference calls and investment conferences a year.
- has a Rolodex full of industry sources.
- has years of full-time money management experience.
- gets every Wall Street research report in seconds.
- gets daily calls from salespeople at thirty-odd Wall Street firms relaying every scrap of information, scuttlebutt or rumor they hear.
- has phone numbers of CEOs, CFOs, etc., on his or her cell phone.
- and, yes, watches CNBC (often howling with laughter).

Are these professionals so talented and well-informed that they can't be beaten? No. In fact, despite these advantages, more than half lose the active management game—usually to other professionals. The efforts of all these professionals do, however, make it harder for *you* to win, a fact that you would be wise to keep in mind.

Those who have a vested interest in your trading often imply that the reason most professionals lag the market is that they are incompetent (implication: you can do better). Sadly, this is absurd. It is similar to suggesting that major league baseball players strike out a lot because they are incompetent. Professional baseball players are not incompetent, and unless you're willing to do the work necessary to become one, you almost certainly can't do better.

Three Advantages You Do Have

Some good news: If you play the money-management game *intelligently*, you will have three potential advantages over most professionals. The first will effortlessly allow you to beat the majority of them. The second and third might even, in rare cases, allow you to beat the market.

Your first advantage—the only one you should pursue unless you are willing to devote your life to the task—is that you don't have to *try* to beat the market. Instead, you can just buy low-cost passive funds. This will guarantee that you will beat most professionals, who are paid to try to beat the market and, therefore, *can't* buy low-cost passive funds. The most client-oriented move for most investment professionals would be to fire themselves and put their clients in index funds. Few will choose this route.

Does buying low-cost index funds sound like a cop-out? Well, here's another way of saying the same thing: After more than a century of research, the world's smartest investment gurus have finally figured out a simple, foolproof way for you to beat the pros. You don't need expertise. You don't need to spend time or money learning complex techniques. You don't have to buy software, hire advisors, or read research. You don't have to worry about making expensive mistakes. You don't have to read a single annual report, make a single forecast or talk to a single customer or employee. The secret? I could tell you, but then Wall Street would have to kill me.

Your second advantage is size. For two reasons, managing a small amount of money is often easier than managing a big one: You have more securities from which to choose, and your transactions will not move the market. The manager of a massive equity fund must restrict purchases to large stocks, because small ones aren't big enough to amount to a meaningful position in the portfolio. Trading large blocks of stock also usually has an adverse impact on the price of the stock, thus reducing a fund's return. Small investors, in contrast, can buy or sell any stock in the market, and their transactions do not usually affect the price.

Your third advantage is that, unlike most professionals, you do not have to answer to impatient, demanding clients. The investment business has become so competitive that managers are now held accountable for performance over absurdly short time frames, such as weeks, months and quarters. A manager who under-performs will quickly get flak, and, if the under-performance continues, will soon get fired. The relentless focus on short-term performance forces managers to balance investment risk with career risk, and, in so doing, goads many talented ones into making low-percentage, short-term bets. Such bets often reduce the manager's odds of beating the market over the long term, and also generate increased transaction, research and tax costs (thus hurting the client two ways). The reality of the money management business, however, is that most clients focus on short-term performance, so most professionals must focus on short-term performance, or else risk damaging their businesses and careers. You, on the other hand, have the luxury of being able to focus on the long term.

A long-term focus lets you take factors like valuation and mean reversion into account. Over short time frames, valuation—a stock's price relative to the underlying company's cash flows—has little impact on what the stock will do. Over the long term, however, valuation matters. Focusing on the long term also allows you to reduce costs and stop worrying about what the market will do next (anyone's guess). Just as important, it allows you to avoid competing with most investors by *playing a different game*—the one, for example, Warren Buffett plays.* Even with this advantage, beating the market will be hard enough that you would almost certainly be better off buying a passive fund. But you will have a better chance of winning than if you try to out-trade Fidelity, et al.

So, yes, it is *possible* to consistently beat professional investors. It is *unlikely* and *difficult*, however. Most professional investors are not stupid or incompetent. And, believe me, they will be *very* happy to compete against you.

---

*In part because Warren Buffett is CEO of his company and in part because he is extraordinarily clear-headed, Warren Buffett can take a longer-term perspective than most institutional investors. This does not make him immune from bouts of crappy relative performance, or the criticism, frustration and ridicule that inevitably accompany them. It just means that he is less exposed to career and business risk than many professionals.

The Vast and Unappreciated Role of Luck

The knowledge that the odds and competition are stacked against you might help you begin to resist the siren song of stock picking, market timing, fund picking and other active management techniques. Every day, however, you will be besieged by news, friends, advisors, would-be advisors, success stories, past performance, advertisements and other influences that will chant the "indexing is for losers" refrain and make you drool at the thought of beating the market. If you are to continue to resist these influences—and, thus, keep your odds of long-term success as high as possible—there are several other things you need to know.

First, it is easy to get fooled into thinking that you and your advisors, friends and fund managers are investment whizzes when you are not because, over short time frames, there is a substantial chance you will beat the market by luck alone. Attributing this to skill instead of to chance can make you overconfident, which, in turn, can lead to all sorts of expensive mistakes. Second, as discussed, there are different definitions of "market," and to determine whether you—or anyone else—is actually skilled you have to use the appropriate one. Third,

---

Who Are You Calling Skilled?

One big risk most investors face is the belief that they are better at assessing investing talent than they really are. For example, imagine a two-person coin-prediction contest in which one participant always chooses "heads" and the other always chooses "tails." If a running score of "prediction skill" is kept over a hundred flips, which of the following patterns do you think is more likely?

1. The lead in the contest will see-saw randomly between one competitor and the other.

2. One competitor will quickly get ahead and stay ahead for most of the contest, thus appearing more skilled.

The second scenario is more likely. Even in a head-to-head game of pure luck, in other words, one player will often appear to have more skill.*

---

calculating accurate investment performance is complicated, and many investors make errors that inflate their returns.

Smart? Skillful? Probably Just Lucky

One of the biggest investment risks you face is your own overconfidence: If you are like most investors, you will think you are more talented at picking stocks, advisors and funds

---

*This example is drawn from the excellent book *Investment Management: Portfolio Diversification, Risk, and Timing—Fact and Fiction* by Robert Hagin. The longer the contest lasts, the more the records will converge, but woe to those who assess skill based on the first few dozen tosses.

than you really are. You will be supported in this belief by the frequency with which you appear to be successful, a frequency that exceeds that of almost all other endeavors in life. Unfortunately, your apparent investment success is probably the result of chance and favorable market odds, not skill.

In an average year, at least a third of active investors should beat the market *by luck alone*. Random subsets of stocks in an index usually have about a 50% chance of beating the index average, so someone who selects stocks randomly should have just under a 50% chance of beating the index (because active managers generate costs, while the market doesn't). This means that the average active investor—and you, if you pick stocks—should outperform the market in, say, four out of ten years, from chance alone.*

It is easy to mistake luck for skill when you have fifty-fifty odds. The odds of making money in the market are much better than, say, the odds of hitting a home run off a Major League pitcher or playing violin in a professional orchestra. Neither of these latter feats is likely to happen randomly, whereas stock market success happens randomly *about half the time* (and more often in a bull market, if success is defined as "making money"). Because the odds in the market can create the illusion of skill, you can often feel talented when you aren't: "See, my fund beat the index the last two years. I told you index funds were for the birds."

---

*This is true if the distribution of returns of stocks within the market follows a normal distribution—i.e., if approximately the same number of stocks perform above the mean as below it. Markets usually exhibit normal distributions, but not always. When they don't, a random selection of stocks can result in the majority of investors performing either above or below the market average.

This phenomenon—mistaking luck for skill—infects every inch of investing. It is also probably responsible for more losses and bankruptcies than any other market force since the dawn of time. No matter how often the concept is repeated, no matter how much evidence is provided to back it up, most people can't accept that much of their investing success is attributable to chance. Other people's? Maybe. Theirs? No way. Intelligent investing, however, depends on your being able to distinguish luck from skill—or at least being able to recognize when it is impossible to do so. And the sooner you get in the habit of doing this the better.

So forget for a moment all of the factors that influence stock prices. Imagine, instead, that the market is a coin. Assemble a thousand people and ask them to predict coin flips. When they protest—coin flipping is unpredictable—lie to them. Say that your coin flips are predictable. Say that some of them, thanks to above average powers of perception, will be able to predict the flips with greater than average frequency. Call for predictions. Flip the coin.

When the coin lands, post the names of the "Good Forecasters" on a scoreboard. Call for new predictions and flip again. And so on. After five flips, the scoreboard should display about thirty people who will have been right five times in a row, along with hundreds who have been right two or three times. If you were to conduct interviews, you would probably find people starting to believe that these people were better-than-average flip predictors, especially the ones who had been "right" every time.

After eight flips, you should have about four people with perfect records left. After nine, two. After ten, one. One person whose powers of prediction are apparently so acute that he has correctly called the coin an astonishing ten times in a row. Assuming his success has been noticed after flips four, five or six, you can imagine the accolades he might now be receiving, especially if, prior to every flip, he has explained the prediction ("The prevailing air currents, combined with the average height of the previous tosses and the average rate of the previous spins, will cause the coin to develop such momentum on the downside that, even if it lands on tails, it will bounce and come up heads . . . "). Everyone will want to know the genius's secrets—especially the poor sod who, via the same probabilities, will have been "wrong" every time.

In truth, of course, this savant isn't good: He is just lucky. From luck alone, one person (or fund manager) in a thousand should correctly predict a fifty-fifty outcome ten times in a row. More important, five hundred of the one thousand should make the "correct" prediction half the time. People can feel plenty smart if they are right half of the time—especially because our brains naturally forget the times we were wrong.

The difference between the stock market and a coin is that the market seems (and is widely thought to be) predictable. Note, however, that like a coin flip, the potential "outcome" of the market in any given period is binary: It can only go up or down. Note that only a tiny fraction of investors are right almost all the time. Note that, to be considered a successful investor, you don't have to be right every time, or even most of the time. And next time you hear someone say that such-and-such a fund manager is obviously talented because he beat the market last year—or next time you feel talented because *you* beat the market last year—remind yourself that a monkey would accomplish this feat almost every other year.

Careful What You Mean by "Market"

When assessing investment skill, yours and others, you also need to be careful about comparing apples and oranges. Most investors compare their performance with that of the S&P 500: If they beat it, they conclude that they're talented; if they lag it, they conclude that—well, they usually conclude that they had bad luck or got bad advice, but that's a different problem. In any case, for many investors, the S&P 500 is a poor benchmark against which to gauge success or failure.

When trying to determine whether you (or a fund manager or advisor) has added value, the "market" is best defined as a group of securities with characteristics similar to the ones you are trading. This might include all the securities in a market, or just a subset of them. U.S. stocks, for example, can be categorized into dozens of different indices—small stocks, large stocks, growth stocks, value stocks, etc.—each of which performs differently in a given time period. A stock picker who invests in small stocks when they are doing relatively well may beat the S&P 500 even if she is a lousy stock picker. The same goes for a manager who buys value (cheap) stocks when they are doing well. Both managers would beat one definition of "the market," but not because of stock picking skill. Rather, they would beat it simply because of the type of stocks they held.*

Why is this important? Because if you compare your performance to the wrong benchmark, you might be fooled into

---

*A case in which it would be the result of skill would be if the portfolio manager was actively switching into and out of subcategories of stocks, trying to time their relative performance. Many portfolio managers try to do this. Few succeed.

thinking that you, your advisor, or your fund managers have above-average skill when you and they don't.

Bear in mind that passive strategies often beat the S&P 500, too. In fact, over the last century, especially in recent years, two passive strategies—one focused on small-cap stocks, the other on cheap ("value") stocks—have thrashed the S&P 500. The "small" and "value" performance advantages, moreover, have also been observed in most other global stock markets over the past century, not just in the United States.

Some researchers, led by Eugene Fama of the University of Chicago and Kenneth French of Dartmouth, argue that the superior performance of small and value stocks is simply required compensation for increased risk, suggesting that the long-term advantage will persist. Others argue that investors consistently underprice small and value stocks. A third view is that the historical premiums are just random fluctuations. Whatever the reason, small and value stocks have beaten the S&P 500 in the past, and many forecasters expect they will continue to in the future. So if your goal is to beat the S&P 500, and you can handle above-market volatility (in the case of small stocks), you may be able to accomplish this with a passive strategy "tilted" toward small and value.*

---

*Bear in mind, however, that even if the superior performance of "small" and "value" stocks persists over the long term, it will likely disappear for years (or even decades) at a time. In the years after the discovery of the small-stock effect, for example, small stocks lagged the broader markets, frustrating those who thought they had stumbled upon a free lunch. There is no free lunch. Even if the small and value premiums persist, they will likely be accompanied by greater risk, so you won't get something for nothing.

U.S. Equity Returns and Risk, by Size, 1926–2005*

	Return	Risk	
Large Company Stocks		10.4%	20.2%
Small Company Stocks	12.6%	32.9%	

U.S. Equity Returns and Risk, by Size and Style, 1969–2005**

	Return	Risk
Growth Stocks	9.2%	19.6%
Value Stocks	11.5%	16.7%
Small Value Stocks	15.3%	21.4%

In any event, because of the small and value premiums, investors who primarily trade such stocks have looked (and felt) like market wizards in recent years, at least when compared to the S&P 500. Investment styles, however, go in and out of vogue. They work for a while, gaining evangelists and adherents, and then they don't work for a while, causing observers

*Source: Ibbotson Associates. Large-company stocks are defined as the S&P 500 for 1957–2005 and S&P 90 for 1926–1956. Small-company stocks are the smallest 20% of companies, ranked by market capitalization. Return is the annualized geometric return over the period. Risk (standard deviation) is the amount by which annual returns have varied around the mean. Approximately two-thirds of years fall within one standard deviation of the mean (for large stocks, 10.4% plus or minus 20.2%), 95% within two standard deviations (10.4% plus or minus 40.4%), and nearly 100% within three.

**Source: Ibbotson Associates. "Value" and "growth" are subjective definitions, usually based on either price-to-earnings or price-to-book value. Ibbotson Associates uses the latter. Return and risk definitions are the same as above.

to conclude that they are kaput. When we enter an inevitable period in which small and value stocks under-perform big and expensive stocks, many investors who have done well in recent years will look (and feel) like bozos.

The best way to measure active management success and skill is to compare the performance of the handpicked portfolio with that of an index comprised *of all stocks with similar characteristics* (aka, a "passive benchmark"). The performance of small-cap investors should be compared to an appropriate small-stock benchmark, the performance of large-stock investors to a large-stock benchmark, etc. Only by doing this can you begin to determine whether you have beaten the market through skill instead of luck (or mismeasurement).

Careful How You Calculate Those Investment Returns

A final word of caution before you take your investment returns as proof that you are a market genius: Make sure you have calculated them correctly.

Remember the Beardstown Ladies? The charming group of senior investors from Beardstown, Illinois, who put the S&P 500 to shame? The Beardstown Ladies validated the 1990s pastime of do-it-yourself stock picking, and their beat-the-pros investment book—*The Beardstown Ladies' Common-Sense Investment Guide: How We Beat the Stock Market—And How You Can, Too*—became an instant, beloved bestseller. At first, the Ladies' ten-year performance did seem amazing: 23% per year, a full eight percentage points better than the S&P 500's 15% return over the same period. It seemed amazing, that is, right up until a sharp reader discovered that it had been miscalculated.

How much did the Beardstown Ladies actually earn from 1984–1993? A tad over 9% per year, fourteen percentage points per year below the return they had claimed and six percentage points below the S&P 500. The cause of the error? A "data input" mistake. A mistake missed by all sixteen women in the investment club, along with the book's publisher, dozens of media outlets, and millions of viewers, readers and listeners. A mistake that prompted the Ladies to sheepishly explain that the real purpose of their club was the "Three E's" (Education, Enjoyment and Enrichment), rather than the "One R" (Return) hyped on the book's cover. A mistake that got the publisher, Hyperion, hit with a lawsuit. And so on.

There were inevitable calls for the Beardstown Ladies to be incarcerated, but most observers recognized (and ridiculed) an honest, if expensive, mistake. And the point here is not to re-bludgeon the investment club. It is simply to illustrate that, when calculating investment returns, it is easy to make mistakes—especially mistakes that make your return look better than it is.*

For example, many people calculate returns by noting how much their account balances have increased or decreased. If no money is ever added to or taken out of the account, this is valid. If money *is* added or taken out, however, the resulting "return" will be wrong. Others try to adjust for fund flows by adding or subtracting the net flow from the account's final value, which also produces an incorrect return: If money was added just before a good stretch (or removed just before a bad one), the return will be inflated. Another common mistake is

---

*It is also worth noting that the Beardstown Ladies would have earned a vastly better return if they had just bought an S&P 500 index fund.

to calculate the average of each annual return and then average these averages. Unfortunately, this gives you an *arithmetic* return, instead of a *geometric* return, which also overstates the compound return.

And then there are the less-mathematical distortions. Some folks don't include their bad stock picks in their return calculations ("Those were just mistakes"), and others ignore transaction costs, advisory fees, and/or taxes. Most investors focus only on returns irrespective of risk. (Roulette winners earn fabulous returns, but this does not indicate investment skill.) And, of course, many investors are eager to tell you about the amazing quarter they just had, while ignoring the seven previous years.

The Trouble with "Cheap" and "Expensive"

Before moving on to the final topic in this four-chapter attempt to dissuade you from trying to beat the market, I want to be clear: I am not to arguing that stock picking and other active management techniques *never* work. I am arguing that, even if they *do* work, for some investors, some of the time, they are difficult and risky enough that it is a mistake for most investors to pursue them. If you are like most investors (and like me), you will be slow to accept this, because it will seem so counter to what you see and hear every day. Thus, you will have to reach the conclusion yourself, through trial, error and research.

At the end of this book, I will include a Further Reading list that I hope will help in the latter effort. If you are like me, you will want to examine each of the dozens of methods by which investors try to beat the market—fundamental analysis, technical analysis, fund-flow analysis, etc.—to see if any work consistently. The simple answer is "no," but you may well want to see the evidence for yourself. (Good news: Most of the studies are available online.) Meanwhile, in this book, I will focus on *one* method of stock picking and market timing—

Why Good Companies Often Make Bad Investments

When describing the challenges of stock picking, advisor and author Larry Swedroe offers the following example. In a horse race, would you bet on a lightning-fast stallion who wins every race—or a gimpy old mare? Given even odds, most people would pick the stallion.

But, of course, in a horse race, the odds won't be even. To make money in horse racing, you have to consistently find the horses whose prospects are overestimated or underestimated by everyone else.

And so it is in the stock market. You can't beat the market by making obvious bets. To win the active management game, you have to determine which companies have brighter futures than the stock market thinks and which companies have dimmer ones, and you have to do a better job of this than thousands of others trying to do the same thing. As at the track, this is easier said than done.

fundamental analysis—with the aim of illustrating why beating the market is so much more difficult than it sounds.

Fundamental Analysis:
At Best, an Educated Guess

No investing advice seems more sound than that you should buy "undervalued" stocks and sell "overvalued" ones. As a result, the most popular school of investment analysis, fundamental analysis, consists of scrutinizing industries, companies and cash flows with the aim of determining what stocks are "worth," so that this "intrinsic value" can be compared with the stock's price. Wall Street, the financial press, and millions of investors devote countless hours and dollars to such analyses.

Professors forever develop more refined valuation techniques. Fanatically precise analysts compute projected earnings to the penny and intrinsic value to the dollar.

Given the common belief that careful fundamental analysis is the definition of wise investing, it is easy to assume that, if one just does the work—studies companies, interviews customers, calculates intrinsic values—success is guaranteed. In fact, as with all stock-picking techniques, success is *unlikely*, in part because thousands of other investors are doing the same work, and in part because there is so much subjective interpretation involved.

The aggregate result for most fundamental investors, in fact, is the usual one: failure. No matter how committed they are to buying cheap stocks and selling expensive ones, most still do worse than they would have done in a value-blind index fund. There are four reasons for this. First, competition is so intense that obvious "mispricings" are quickly spotted and bought or sold away. Second, performing detailed fundamental analysis costs money. Third, determining whether a stock is cheap or expensive can actually be quite difficult. Fourth, just because a stock is under- or overpriced doesn't mean it will regress to its intrinsic value anytime soon.

To appreciate the latter reasons, it helps to review some basic valuation theory and walk through a simple example.

Intrinsic Value: An Argument, Not a Fact

A share of stock is, in theory, worth the present value of the future cash flows that will accrue to that share. (In practice, a share is worth what someone will pay for it, a fact that wise analysts always remember.) Given the confidence with which some commentators state this theory, a casual observer might assume that the "present value of future cash flows" is an indisputable number, akin to a price tag on a can of soup. In reality, it is not a number but an argument, and, in most cases, it is a surprisingly imprecise argument, with a wide range of reasonable conclusions.

An estimate of the "present value of future cash flows" requires, at minimum, two assumptions: 1) an estimate of the future cash flows, and 2) an appropriate discount rate. Most cash-flow projections extend only five or ten years, moreover, so valuation analyses also usually require a third assumption: 3) a "terminal multiple" to value the company's operations beyond the forecast period. These terms can be confusing, so here's a quick explanation:

A "discount rate" is a tool with which to estimate the current value of money to be received in the future. Thanks to inflation, risk, and opportunity cost, a dollar you expect to receive in a year is worth less than a dollar you have today. With 3% inflation, for example, today's dollar will be worth ninety-seven cents in a year, and there is always a chance that it will never materialize (if, for example, the company you invested in goes bankrupt). And then there is the money you will sacrifice by not investing today's dollar in a risk-free investment for a year. All of these factors reduce the value of money you expect to receive in the future, and they are all factored into the discount rate (which is sometimes also called the "required rate of return").

A "terminal multiple" allows the analyst to estimate the value of cash flows to be received after the explicit forecast period. Most successful companies won't suddenly stop generating cash in five or ten years; rather, they will keep generating it in perpetuity. To relieve the analyst of the burden of projecting hundreds of years of performance, the cash flows beyond the forecast period are usually valued with a terminal multiple.

Lastly, what is a "cash flow"? Strictly speaking, in this context, it is a dividend—actual money distributed to the owner of the share. Because many companies do not pay dividends, however, and because dividend policies often change, most investors treat "cash flow" as synonymous with "earnings."* Most cash-flow projections extend only five or ten years, so valuation analyses also usually require a "terminal multiple" to value the company's operations beyond the forecast period. Once one has these assumptions—cash flows, discount rate, and terminal multiple—estimating present value is a matter of math.

However:

1. No one really knows what the future cash flows will be.
2. Discount rates and terminal multiples are subjective assumptions based on the prices of other securities (and, consequently, change as the prices of the other securities change).
3. Small tweaks in assumptions can yield big changes in estimated value.

To illustrate this, let's assume that we know that a company will earn $1 per share per year forever. In this case, all we need to determine the present value of future cash flows is a discount rate. Because the cash flows are known, we can use the so-called "risk-free" rate, the rate of return that an investor can earn without risking a loss of capital. A proxy for the risk-free

---

*That earnings are not, in fact, cash flows to shareholders, and that many shareholders never receive so much as a dime from their stocks until they sell them, renders most valuation assessments academic (and based on flawed theory, to boot).

rate is the yield on ten-year Treasury bonds, which, recently, was about 4.2%. Discount 150 years of earnings of $1 a year (the financial equivalent of "forever") at this rate and—voila!—the value of our hypothetical stock is about $24. If the stock is trading at $20, we have apparently found ourselves a bargain.

But what if we assume that the risk-free rate will change, as it undoubtedly will? What if, for example, we assume that the yield on ten-year Treasury bonds will eventually regress to its long-term mean of about 7%, a scenario that, given enough time, is probable? Well, then our $24 stock would only be worth $14—suggesting that, at $20, it is *overvalued*. Or what if the risk-free rate jumps to 10% or more, as in the inflation crisis of the early 1980s? Then the stock will be worth less than $10. In other words, even if we know for a fact that a company will earn $1 per share per year forever—something that, in practice, we will never come close to knowing—we might conclude that the stock's "intrinsic value" is anywhere from less than $10 to more than $30 (the risk-free rate could always drop, too), with a central value around $14, the value generated using the bond's long-term mean. Twenty dollars might not be such a bargain, after all.

Impact of Discount Rate Assumption
Value of $1 Per Year for 150 Years

Cash Flow	Years	Discount Rate	Present Value
$1	150	4.2%	$24
$1	150	7%	$14
$1	150	3%	$33

As subjective as the choice of a discount rate is, moreover, it is the most objective assumption in a valuation analysis. The *most subjective* assumption, meanwhile, is the estimate of future cash flows.

What will, say, Google's cash flows be over the next 150 years? Well, if the company continues on its early trajectory— if it survives challenges from Microsoft, Yahoo!, and legions of hungry start-ups; if it proves to be not only "the next Microsoft" but "the next GE" (a company that has existed for more than a century); if its extraordinary profit margins remain intact—then Google's cash flows might grow steadily in perpetuity. On the other hand, if Google stumbles—if its founders get bored; if the industry changes; if competitors adapt—then Google might look more like Digital Equipment Corporation, a successful company that dominated its industry for a while before becoming roadkill. Plug this range of cash flows into your Google valuation analysis, and it is not hard to conclude that Google's stock could be "worth" anywhere from under a hundred to a couple of thousand dollars a share. Valuing a high-risk, high-growth stock like Google is more subjective than valuing, say, a mature utility, but even in the latter case, analysts who think they can pinpoint stock values are hallucinating.

The Other Problem:
Getting the Market to Agree and/or Care

This brings us to the second problem with valuation: Its lack of relevance as an intermediate-term price prediction tool. Even if we could establish for certain what a stock was worth, which we can't, this would be no guarantee that the stock would trade there in any reasonable time frame (or ever). The only thing that would make the stock trade there would be enough other investors buying or selling it to drive the price there, a process that might take years (over which the stock's intrinsic value would almost certainly change).

Unfortunately for fundamental analysts, investors buy and sell stocks for dozens of reasons, many of which have nothing to do with valuation (for example, portfolio rebalancing, fund redemptions or inflows, technical or quantitative analyses, hedging and arbitrage). These transactions make stock prices move, whether or not the movements are "justified" in the opinion of a fundamental analyst. Even if the fundamental analyst concludes that the market has gone stark raving mad, in fact, this will not necessarily allow him to make money (or stop him from losing it). As John Maynard Keynes is said to have put it, the market can stay irrational longer than you can stay solvent.

Think the Market's Undervalued?
Get Ready to Wait for Godot

Over the long haul, valuation does matter: The market is not random, market prices do tend to regress to long-term means, and long-term investors are better off buying when stocks are cheap. As discussed, however, the "long term" can mean decades, and valuation is not a particularly helpful prediction tool over short-term time frames (not worthless—just not particularly helpful). Also, long-term averages and intrinsic values are easier to establish for diversified markets than they are for individual stocks, especially in fast-growing sectors like emerging technology.

Even with markets, moreover, valuation is not a particularly good price prediction tool. Take the S&P 500, for example, an index that can be viewed as a single stock whose

The Right Way to Value the Market

It's true: It is better for everyone if the market goes up. Better for investors, better for Wall Street, better for the financial media, better for the economy, better for job-seekers, better for retirees, better for national morale. It's also true that the market *usually* goes up, so being bullish is not only a way to root for the popular team, it is a way to play the odds. Unfortunately, these realities lead to what economists Andrew Smithers and Stephen Wright describe as "a large amount of nonsense that is written about [stock market] value," and, specifically, "a demand for measures of valuation that can be used to claim that the stock market is always cheap."

What valuation measures are "nonsense"? The standard price-earnings ratio, for one. Most strategists calculate the market P-E by dividing the market's price by its current- or forward-year earnings. Unfortunately, this can create a misleading picture of value. The level of earnings depends to a large extent on the business cycle: in good times, earnings are high (and, thus, P-Es are low), and, in bad times, earnings are low (and P-Es are high). Investors who focus on

valuation is tied to the cash flows of the biggest companies in the U.S. economy. A glance at history reveals that the S&P 500's price often takes eons to regress to its long-term mean.

According to data compiled by Yale professor Robert Shiller, from 1881 to 2000 the S&P 500's average price-earnings ratio was about sixteen times earnings, with a peak of forty-four times (1999) and a trough of five times (1920). From this data, one might conclude that the average value of the S&P 500 is about sixteen times earnings, and, therefore, in years when prices are significantly below or above this level, stocks are "cheap" or "expensive." Judging from the eventual performance single-year P-Es, therefore, can conclude that the market is expensive when it is cheap, and vice versa.

Another bogus valuation metric? The bond yield-earnings yield ratio, often referred to as the "Fed Model." This holds that when the market's earnings yield (earnings divided by price) is higher than the yield on Treasury bonds, stocks are cheap, and vice versa. In recent history, this measure has appeared to have some predictive value. A glance at broader history, however, reveals that the recent correlation is a coincidence. The yield ratio, Smithers and Wright conclude, "is a criterion of particular charm in that it appears to be virtually indefensible. It is without any support from economic theory, nor can it be defended by looking at the statistical evidence."

What valuation measures actually have predictive value? The "cyclically adjusted P-E," which compares the market's price to an average of several years of earnings (thus, minimizing the impact of the business cycle), and something called "Tobin's Q," which is a measure of replacement cost. At this writing, both measures suggest that the U.S. stock market is still expensive.

of the index, this would have been right. It would not, however, have allowed one to predict with confidence what the S&P 500 was going to do over the *following* year or two.

In 1970, for example, the S&P 500 dropped below sixteen times earnings for the first time since 1958. This apparent undervaluation did not, however, signal that prices were about to go up. In fact, twelve years later, in 1982, the index was trading at an even lower valuation, about seven times earnings, and it did not return to "fair value" until 1986, sixteen years later. Similarly, in 1986, if one had decided to sell the S&P 500 on the theory that over sixteen times earnings was "overvalued," one would soon have torn more hair out. The S&P 500 has remained above sixteen times earnings since 1987. Those who refused to pay more than "fair value" missed twenty years of a major bull market.*

The Least-Bad Market Prediction Tool

If assessing whether stocks are "cheap" or "expensive" isn't much help in determining what the market will do next, what is? As it turns out, almost nothing. But here's a look at what might be described as the "least-bad" market prediction tool.

Richard Bernstein, the chief U.S. strategist at Merrill Lynch, has tested the effectiveness of several metrics commonly used to predict the performance of the market over horizons of up to one year, including price-earnings ratios, the slope of the yield curve, changes in interest rates and several so-called "sentiment indicators," which measure the relative optimism or pessimism of investors and analysts. Of these, the most effective is not p-e ratios or other common valuation tools, but a sentiment indicator of Bernstein's own invention—the "sell-side indicator."**

---

*A market strategist might argue that the S&P 500 is only "worth" sixteen times earnings when other valuation metrics (namely, interest rates) are at a particular level. The problem with this argument as a forecasting tool is that to predict what the market will do, the analyst must also predict what the price of another asset will do.

**On Wall Street, brokerage firms are referred to as the "sell side" and institutional investors are referred to as the "buy side." In the normal course of business, brokerage firms do not sell stocks so much as help the institutions trade them (buy or sell). When a brokerage firm raises money for a company or government, however, it does sell securities. This is where the terms "sell side" and "buy side" come from.

The sell-side indicator measures the consensus outlook of Wall Street strategists, as determined by their recommended asset-allocation models (recommendations about what percentage of the portfolio the average investor should place in stocks, bonds and cash). Bernstein assumes that, when strategists place a high percentage of their model portfolios in stocks, they are optimistic about future stock performance, and vice versa. The sell-side indicator averages the strategists' recommendations and then plots the result on a chart tracking their relative optimism or pessimism over time.

Wall Street strategists are highly trained professionals with decades of experience, so when they think the market is going to go up, it's probably going to go up—right? Well, no. The sell-side indicator, like some other sentiment indicators, is a "contrarian" indicator: It holds that when Wall Street strategists are most confident the market is going to rise, it is most likely to fall, and vice versa. The idea behind contrarian indicators is that analysts and investors put their money where their mouths are: When they think the market is going up, they own stocks, and when they think it is going down, they don't (and if they don't, people who listen to them do). What causes movements in stock prices is not absolute demand but changes in demand, so when everyone is already bullish, there are few people left to get bullish. Extreme bullishness, in other words, triggers a "sell" signal, and extreme bearishness, a "buy."

According to Bernstein, over the last twenty years, the sell-side indicator has predicted about 33% of the variability of future S&P 500 returns, a level significantly higher than p-e ratios (14%) interest rates (4%) and other popular metrics. For example, Wall Street strategists were most bearish about stocks in 1989 (S&P 500 up 27% the following year); 1995

(S&P 500 up 34%, 20%, and 31% the next three years); and 1997 (S&P 500 up 27% and 20% the next two years). Similarly, strategists were most bullish about stocks in 2000 and 2001, at the beginning of the worst bear market since the 1970s.

Commentators love to use measures like the sell-side indicator to suggest that Wall Street strategists are idiots. The intelligent takeaways, however, are more profound. First, Wall Street strategists are the furthest thing from idiots; they are smart, well-educated, well-informed and well-trained professionals, and they still often get it wrong (so you can imagine the result for most people, who are relatively inexperienced, untrained and uninformed). Second, almost all of us, professionals and amateurs alike, form expectations about the future by assessing what has happened in the recent past, by looking in the "rearview mirror." Consequently, we are most bullish when we should be most bearish (at the end of long bull markets) and most bearish when we should be most bullish (at the end of long bear markets).

Third, the sell-side indicator is Richard Bernstein's best prediction tool—and it is far from perfect. The indicator was wrong in 2003, for example, and wrong in the last years of the 1990s. The lesson here is that predicting the market's movements over one- to three-year time frames is difficult—so difficult that, no matter what tools they use, only a small percentage of investors can do it with an accuracy that exceeds that of luck. And the lesson of that, unfortunately, is that the vast majority of the effort devoted to trying to predict what the market is going to do next is a waste of time.

A Final Plug for Passive

To most investors, the last few chapters will sound like heresy. Most investors believe—or act as though—trying to pick winners is the definition of intelligent investing. After all, Warren Buffett picks winners. Peter Lynch picked winners. Warren Buffett's mentor, Benjamin Graham, picked winners—and wrote two enduring classics about how to do it called *Security Analysis* and *The Intelligent Investor*. Even *I* used to pick winners (until I picked some losers, too, and blew myself up).

The goal of most research and advice produced by Wall Street and the investment media, moreover, is to help investors try to pick winners. This, however, is not because active management is a wise strategy. Rather, it is because most investors are active investors (preach to the choir, give your customers, readers, or viewers what they want) and because—for Wall Street and the investment media—active management is more profitable than passive management. It is also because passive management is still a relatively new concept. John Bogle, the founder of Vanguard and one of the true heroes of individual investing, started the first index fund about thirty years ago. Speculation, meanwhile, as 1920s market wizard Jesse Livermore pointed out, is as old as the hills.

Because active management is the bread and butter of Wall Street and the investment media, you hear less about the supremacy of passive management than you should. Aside from an occasional article observing that, as usual, passive index funds have beaten most active funds—often accompanied by the incorrect conclusion that this is a temporary and embarrassing aberration—Wall Street and the investment media either don't mention the poor odds of active management or encourage investors to think they will defy them. Because most of us believe that we are better than average, we are a receptive audience.

Hopefully, the poor performance of active investors—individuals and professionals alike—will help persuade you (as it did me) that, for most intelligent investors, passive investing is the wise choice. Still, no matter how much you learn about the past performance of *other* investors, you will probably believe that you are the exception, and you will probably go on believing this until you are proven wrong (and are poorer for it). I would respectfully suggest that it would be wise to assume *first* that you are *not* the exception, but I know this is asking a lot.

Ultimately, whether you choose an active or passive strategy will likely have a smaller impact on your returns than your ability to reduce your investment costs and manage your own dangerous emotions. Holding a diversified portfolio of active funds will likely cost you a pretty penny over your lifetime, but the loss will be nothing compared to the fortune you will lose if you ignore costs, trade frequently, try to time the market, take too much or too little risk, chase returns or otherwise act like the average investor.

Summary: Why Passive Wins

There are dozens of ways to pick stocks and time the market. Some work for some people and don't work for others. Some work for a while and then stop working. Some work in some markets but not in others. Some never work. In my experience, most investors keep trying active-management strategies until they find one that works, use it until it stops working, and then try to find another. After repeating this process many times, the investors either retire (richer if they were managing other people's money, poorer if they were managing their own) or become passive investors.

Passive investing, meanwhile, works in all markets (relative to active investing). It also works for all investors. Passive managers don't devote much time to analyzing companies, cash flows and intrinsic values. More importantly, they don't devote *any* time to trying to predict the future. Instead, they establish quantitative criteria and then buy groups of stocks that meet the criteria; in some cases, these criteria are as simple as "all the stocks in the market"; in others, they involve complex fundamental and price screens. Again, on its face, this sounds like a terrible idea—they buy the dogs, too?—but it has several practical benefits.

- First, it is harder to distinguish between "winners" and "dogs" than most people think (except, of course, in hindsight, when everyone is Warren Buffett). A stock that looks like a dog to you usually looks like a dog to everyone else, too. All that pessimism will drive the stock's price so low that the company will often exceed expectations, which will drive the price up. Similarly, a stock that looks like a winner to you will be on others' "buy" lists, as well. All the buying will drive its price so high that the underlying company will often fail to meet expectations, which will drive the price down.
- Second, passive investing does not depend on prophecies about the future. Thus, it eliminates much of the uncertainty that plagues fundamental analysis and other active management techniques.
- Third, passive investing reduces the potential for human error—specifically, the tendency to get seduced by

exciting stories, charismatic managers, past performance, peer pressure, fear and greed.

- Fourth, passive investing reduces subjective interpretation, another by-product of the human condition. Depending on who is looking, a stock's glass will always be half-full or half-empty, and there is no reliable way to tell which is which.

- Fifth, passive investors do not compete with anyone, and, therefore, do not have to beat anyone. True, they sacrifice the opportunity to hit game-winning home runs. But they also don't strike out.

- Lastly, passive management avoids the considerable costs of active management (MBAs, business class travel, five-star hotels, third-party research, transaction costs, short-term tax costs, etc.). Your net return will always equal your gross return minus your costs, so, all else being equal, lower costs mean higher returns.

In short, winning the active-management game is much harder than most people think. This doesn't mean you are nuts to play it. It does mean, however, that you should be aware of how likely you are to lose.

By the way, did you know that the dean of fundamental analysis, Benjamin Graham, eventually changed his mind about the wisdom of trying to pick winners through painstaking analyses? In 1976, shortly before his death, the man who has (so far) taught three generations of fundamental analysts how to practice their craft, had this to say:

I am no longer an advocate of elaborate techniques of security analysis in order to find superior value opportunities. This was a rewarding activity, say, 40 years ago, when [the bible of fundamental analysis, Graham and Dodd's *Security Analysis*] was first published; but the situation has changed. I doubt whether such extensive efforts will generate sufficiently superior selections to justify their cost.*

What did Graham mean when he said "the situation has changed?" He didn't elaborate, but several reasons leap to mind.

First, in the last seventy years, the stock market has gone from being dominated by amateur investors to full-time professionals, a shift that has only become more pronounced in the last thirty years. One result of this is that "mis-pricings" that went unnoticed for months back in Graham's early years are now discovered and exploited in minutes. Second, the amount and quality of information available about the most obscure public security today dwarfs that available about even the bellwethers a half-century ago, making it harder for investors to dig up facts that other investors don't know. Third, instead of being published on wood pulp, in limited quantities, and made available only to those with the time, inclination and shoe leather to find it, information is now transmitted instantly via text, conference calls, radio, television, video and global information services, everywhere in the world.

---

*This quote is occasionally used to suggest that Graham completely repudiated his former work by suggesting that stock analysis was worthless. In fact, he just sounded like a modern-day passive investor. He advocated screening stocks using simple valuation and fundamental criteria and then buying large groups of them—a methodology similar to that used by passive value funds. What Graham did "recant" was the idea that by studying companies in detail, one could identify a few individual opportunities that could constitute the entire portfolio.

Fourth, the moment new information hits the public eye, it is dissected, discussed and debated by thousands of analysts, amateur and professional alike, through all of the same electronic channels, until most reasonable conclusions that can be drawn from it have been. Fifth, many forms of information that used to be quite valuable—material *non-public* information, for example—are now illegal to trade on, and modern record-keeping has allowed regulators to put the fear of God in anyone tempted to use them. Sixth, mind-boggling technology advances now allow even part-time investors to screen tens of thousands of securities in dozens of markets on multiple continents in the time it would have taken an early Graham-era analyst to compute the "net current assets" of a single company.*

Seventh, and most importantly, the establishment of market information and research centers such as the Center for Research in Security Prices (CSRP) has allowed brilliant analysts in both the public and private sectors to study markets and investing in ways that the young Benjamin Graham could only have dreamed of—and, in so doing, to assemble a body of knowledge that makes much of the "investment wisdom" of the 1920s and 1930s seem as rudimentary as early twentieth century medicine. As Graham well knew, human nature drives much market behavior, and human nature will never change. As in other fields, however, investment knowledge has pro-

---

*Think about it: When Graham and Dodd wrote *Security Analysis* in 1934, there was no Internet. There were no spreadsheets, computers, or information databases. There weren't even any *calculators*. There were no company conference calls or quarterly earnings releases. There were few filing requirements, lax accounting rules, little legal enforcement. There were only a handful of mutual funds, no hedge funds and no computerized trading. There was no CNBC, no market radio, no Bloomberg, no Yahoo! Finance, no real-time quotes. There were *paper tickers*, for God's sake.

gressed significantly, and, slowly but surely, it is changing the definition of intelligent investing.

Benjamin Graham was a smart, brave man, one confident enough to admit that some of the strategies and ideas that had made him famous were no longer relevant. The trends that produced what he saw in the 1970s—a world that had changed considerably in forty years—have only accelerated in the last three decades. Without presuming to put words in the master's mouth, one can imagine that if Graham were to re-write *The Intelligent Investor* today, having digested the work of William Sharpe, Eugene Fama, Kenneth French, Burton Malkiel, Mark Carhart and dozens of other researchers, he might have some different things to say.

Serenity Prayer for the Intelligent Investor

Even if you can't beat the market, you can be a wiser, happier investor. How? By invoking the Investor's Serenity Prayer: Accept what you can't know or control, know and control what you can and get wise enough to tell the difference. If you don't, your investing life will be an endless series of dreamy infatuations, dashed hopes and lingering resentments.

Here's what you can't know or control:

- What the market will do
- What a stock, bond, or company will do
- What your mutual fund will do
- What interest rates will do
- What inflation will do
- What the dollar will do
- What the economy will do
- What the Fed will do
- What everyone else will do

Here's what you can know and control:

- Diversification
- Costs

Obvious? Perhaps. Judging from the way most investors spend their time and energy, though, you would think it was the theory of relativity.

Here's the only honest answer to the questions the world struggles with daily about what stocks, bonds, mutual funds, interest rates, inflation, the dollar, the economy, the government and other investors are going to do:

"No one knows."

Really. A persistent myth among Wall Street outsiders is that, somewhere, there's a Wall Street insider who *knows*. I have been as far inside Wall Street as it is possible to get, and I can assure you that the only people who *know* have information that is illegal to trade on. Most of these questions are simply unanswerable, and always will be, no matter how much research and analysis you do. The best the smartest insiders can do—the best *anyone* can do—is develop answers that are right *more often* than the average answer. Therefore, unless you're willing to devote your life to the study of such questions—and, in most cases, even then—here's the wisest attitude for you to have:

"I don't know, and I don't care."

How can you have such an attitude in the face of such monumental uncertainty? By ignoring what you can't know or control and focusing on what you can. Doing so is not the equivalent of stuffing your head in the sand. Rather (with thanks to Rudyard Kipling), it is the equivalent of keeping your head when everyone else has long since lost theirs. If you diversify well and control your costs, you should do okay no matter what happens.

Job 1: Diversify

D-I-V-E-R-S-I-F-Y. The mere sound of the word causes people to nod off. Instead of the life-changing romance of winning the lottery, it suggests boredom, plodding and single-digit returns. Diversifying well is more challenging than you think, though, and the opportunity for endless refinements can keep you busy for the rest of your days. Intelligent diversification will allow you to achieve an appropriate level of expected risk and return, and reduce the risk of permanently losing your shirt. For most of us, this last feature is the clincher.

The point of diversification is to own investments that 1) have a positive expected real return, and 2) fluctuate somewhat independently of one another (investments that have low correlation, as the academics say). This way, when one investment is doing badly, another might be doing well, and vice versa. Diversification cannot eliminate risk. It can, however, reduce the risk required to generate a particular return.

What Diversification Is Not

Appropriate diversification depends on your circumstances and risk tolerance. Losses tolerable for one investor will plunge another into the pit of despair, so one size doesn't fit all. Many people who think they are adequately diversified aren't, so let's start with a look at what adequate diversification almost certainly is not:

- *Owning twenty technology stocks*: Better than owning one or two, but not much better. Stocks in the same industry usually trade like schools of fish.

- *Owning three oil stocks, two bank stocks, one biotech stock mentioned on CNBC last week and three of the "Ten Hot Stocks for 2007"*: Leaving aside the dubiousness of your stock-picking strategy, adequate diversification in a single market usually means owning about fifty stocks in dozens of industries.

- *Owning cash and Treasury bonds*: Fine for the short term, but over the long term, inflation, taxes, low returns and rising interest rates could kill you.

- *Owning some U.S. stock funds*: Probably enough diversification within "U.S. equities," but if the U.S. stock market tanks, you're hosed.

- *Using one investment advisor or firm*: No one's perfect, and competition never hurts. Also, banks, brokerage firms and IT systems have been known to fail, and even charming advisors occasionally blow it or abscond with your loot.

- *Keeping your 401K in "what you know"—your company's stock*: Please, please, please don't do this. Unless you are the CFO of your company, you really *don't* know. Also, you already depend on your company for your most important financial asset: Your job.

- *Never exercising your employee stock options because Warren Buffett and Bill Gates didn't sell Berkshire Hathaway and Microsoft, respectively*: Most companies, sadly, aren't Berkshire Hathaway and Microsoft. Most employees, meanwhile, aren't CEOs. And any employee who keeps his entire net worth tied up in a single company is frighteningly concentrated.

- *Exercising your stock options and keeping the stock to avoid paying short-term capital gains tax*: A favorite in the late

1990s, this is often one of the dumbest moves you can make.* Don't be a pig.

- *Investing everything in Berkshire Hathaway because Warren Buffett is God*: Warren Buffett is a god, but he'll also probably die eventually, and, even if he doesn't, keeping all your money in a single stock is nuts.

What Diversification Is

There are two primary drivers of diversification: asset mix and time. In general, the more asset classes you hold, the less volatile your portfolio will be. Similarly, the longer you hold your portfolio, the less your return will vary from the expected long-term mean.

To get the full benefits of diversification, the assets you hold must be *mean-reverting*: No matter how volatile the monthly and yearly returns, they must eventually gravitate toward a long-term average. Major asset classes, such as U.S. stocks, are (or, at least, have been) mean-reverting: Long periods of ex-

---

*Most incentive stock options are exercised through what is known as a "cashless" exercise: Stock purchased with the option is immediately sold, and the employee keeps the difference between the strike price and the exercise price. To avoid paying short-term gains taxes, the employee has to exercise the option and then hold the stock. To do this, he or she has to fork over cash to buy the stock—value that is at risk if the stock drops. If the stock rises over the course of the year, the employee will indeed save the difference between short-term and long-term gains taxes (the point of the strategy). If the stock drops during this period, however, as the stocks of many high-tech and option-intensive companies often do, the employee will end up losing money. Exercising an option and holding the stock is the same as investing in the stock. For an employee, this can be extremely risky. If the stock tanks, it will probably tank for a reason, one that could also cost you your job.

traordinary returns (15%–20% annually) have been followed by long periods of subpar returns (0%–5%), and, taken together, they have produced the familiar 10% mean. The same holds true for bonds, bills, real estate and other major asset classes.

Individual stocks and bonds, meanwhile, are *not* necessarily mean-reverting: Periods of extraordinary returns have been followed by periods of lousy returns, including, sometimes, bankruptcy. Investors who allocated a chunk of their portfolios to Polaroid, Xerox, Digital Equipment Corporation, Enron, Worldcom, Kodak, GM, Ford, AT&T and many other (once) sure-things did not get the same diversification benefit as investors who allocated the same chunk to broad-based mutual funds. Although it is obvious now that these companies were headed for trouble, it was not obvious ahead of time (which is why the stock prices were high). Similarly, it is not obvious today which of the 500 S&P stocks will out-perform the index for the next fifty years—and which will go to zero.

You cannot know for certain that an investment is mean-reverting, but the more securities you hold, the more you will reduce the risk of loss from any one security. The more asset classes you hold, meanwhile, the more you will reduce the risk of loss from any one asset class. And the longer you hold your portfolio, the more you will reduce the risk that your average return will be significantly different than the long-term mean.

How to Build a Portfolio

There are two ways to build a portfolio: from the top down and the bottom up. In the top-down method, you start by dividing your money among different asset classes (stocks, bonds, real estate, etc.), and gradually move toward individual opportunities (funds or securities). In the bottom-up method, you do the reverse: You pick securities or funds until you've invested all your money and—voila!—you have a portfolio.

There's only one *right* way to build a portfolio, however, and that's top down. With this method, you spend the majority of your time and energy on the most important decision: asset allocation. In the bottom-up method, meanwhile, you spend most of your time and energy on the *least* important decisions, such as stock picking. A fund manager can build a portfolio using bottom-up security analysis because someone else (you or your investment advisor) has already made the top-down asset allocation decisions. Unless you really know what you are doing, however, you should *never* build your portfolio from the bottom up.

If this sounds unfamiliar, it is because top-down asset allocation is one of the least dynamic aspects of the market show—which is to say the most stable, least controversial and least transaction-oriented. It is also, therefore, the least *newsworthy*. To stay in business, Wall Street and the investment media need to focus on what has changed and will change, not what is the same. Because intelligent investment policy almost never changes, this creates a conflict. Thankfully (for Wall Street and the investment media), the prices of assets and the fundamentals of companies and the economy constantly change, and this provides an endless flow of material to research, write and talk about.

Put differently, humans operate in different time frames than markets. As a result, we often make investment decisions based on distracting headlines instead of long-standing knowledge. What you read about in the newspaper, watch on CNBC or hear from your friends may be interesting, but it is what you should spend the *least* amount of your investment attention worrying about. This is not just because the investment media is, for its own reasons, obsessed with short-term noise. It is because, assuming your portfolio is adequately diversified, your asset allocation decisions are more important than your security selection decisions. In a diversified portfolio, asset allocation—the percentage of a portfolio devoted to stocks, bonds, cash, real estate and other asset classes—is the largest single contributor to portfolio performance. All else being equal, therefore, you should devote most of your investing effort to allocating your assets appropriately.

So, true diversification means building your portfolio from the top down, starting with asset allocation. It also means reducing exposure to any single asset class, so that you don't get obliterated by crashes. David Swensen, Yale University's outstanding chief investment officer, recommends focusing on six asset classes, all of which can be bought cheaply through low-cost passive funds.

- U.S. stocks
- International developed market stocks
- Emerging market stocks
- U.S. Treasury bonds and bills
- U.S. inflation-protected Treasury bonds (TIPS)
- Real estate investment trusts (REITs)

Swensen recommends that no asset class account for more than 30% of the portfolio or less than 5%. Other experts are more flexible. In any case, the percentage you hold of each asset class should vary depending on your age, risk tolerance, impending cash needs and, possibly, asset price levels. (When the U.S. stock market is extremely expensive, for example, you might reduce your target allocation to U.S. stocks.)* If you need all the money within five years, you should keep most of it in cash. If you don't need any of it for thirty years, you should keep most of it in stocks.

In recent years, as both the U.S. stock and bond markets have delivered disappointing returns, investors and advisors have trumpeted the merits of other asset classes, such as commodities. Although diversified baskets of commodities assembled through the futures markets (oil, gas, soy beans, pork bellies, etc.) have performed well lately, commodities differ from other major asset classes in one important respect: Investing in them is a zero-sum game. The only way you can make money in commodities is by outsmarting those on the other side of your trades. This is not the case with the stock market, which provides its owners with returns of, on average, 10% a year.

Academics argue about whether commodities actually provide true diversification benefits—a positive real return and a reduction of overall portfolio risk—but, with the stock market treading water and inflation picking up, many advisors and pundits have decided that every investor should own a commodity fund. Should you? If it makes you feel better, allocate a small percentage of your portfolio to one. Just don't be sur-

---

*As you probably noticed, this would be a form of active management. I no longer regard valuation as being a particularly helpful tool in predicting near-term price direction, but I am still persuaded by the work of Yale professor Robert Shiller, economist Andrew Smithers, money manager Jeremy Grantham, and others that, over the long term, market valuations do regress to means. Thus, it seems sensible to *modestly* adjust target asset allocations based on valuation extremes (overweighting asset classes that are very cheap and underweighting those that are very expensive). If, eventually, I am persuaded that doing so is worthless or harmful, I'll abandon the practice. In the meantime, it still seems sensible. Old habits die hard.

prised when commodities go out of vogue (read: perform poorly), and your advisor concludes that there's no need to own them.

Also popular for diversification are hedge funds, absolute return funds, private equity funds, venture capital funds funds of funds and other "alternative investments." For obvious reasons, these are appealing. As usual, however, there's a catch. As I'll describe in more detail later, these vehicles simply provide another way to own the same old asset classes. If the U.S. equity market crashes, many equity hedge funds will go down with it.

What Diversification Does

The goal of diversification is to achieve the appropriate balance of risk and return. So, what sorts of returns can you expect in diversified portfolios? And what sorts of risk?

The most common measure of investment risk is standard deviation: The amount each annual or monthly return varies around the long-term average. When returns display what statisticians call "normal distributions," as those of broad markets, mutual funds and well-diversified portfolios tend to, standard deviation provides a reasonable picture of risk.

The S&P 500, for example, has a long-term return of about 10% and a standard deviation of 20%. This means that approximately two-thirds of annual S&P 500 returns have been within twenty percentage points of the 10% average, or between +30% and −10%. Approximately 95% of returns, meanwhile, have been within *two* standard deviations of the mean (+50% and −40%), and approximately 99.7% of returns have been within three standard deviations (+70% and −60%).

The holder of an S&P 500 fund benefits from diversification within a single asset class: The failure of Enron, Worldcom and other companies barely scratched those who held S&P 500 funds. Even so, with a standard deviation of 20%, the S&P 500 is still quite risky. Unless investors are intellectually *and* emotionally committed to holding their portfolios for many years, few would be comfortable with losing more than a third of their portfolio value in one year every twenty years. As a result, for most investors, adequate diversification means combining multiple asset classes.

An advisory firm called Index Funds Advisors has constructed twenty portfolios that span a full spectrum of risk using index funds tied to most major asset classes (excluding commodities and TIPS). In its stock allocations, IFA uses a technique I alluded to earlier, emphasizing small and value stocks to try to exceed the performance of the S&P 500. Otherwise, the components of the IFA portfolios are standard fare.

IFA's portfolios range from a tortoise-like mix dominated by 85% bonds to a hare-like one with 95% stocks. The former is for folks with little income and short-time horizons who can't tolerate risk. The latter is for twenty- or thirty-somethings who make piles of money, won't panic when they temporarily lose their shirts and won't need their savings for decades. Even the latter portfolio is less risky than one composed of only a few blue-chips, or, worse, the stock of your employer. In fact, it is only as risky as the S&P 500.

IFA "Ivory" Portfolio (Most Conservative)

Asset Mix: 85% cash and bonds, 9% U.S. stocks, 3% international stocks, 1.5% emerging markets stocks, 1.5% REITs

Period: 1956–2005

Average Annualized Return: 7%

Risk (Standard Deviation):   3%   (S&P 500 is 20%)

Best 1-Year Annual Return:	23% (1982–1983)
Worst 1-Year Annual Return:	–2% (1969–1970)
Best 5-Year Annual Return:	15% (1981–1986)
Worst 5-Year Annual Return:	3% (1955–1959)
Best 25-Year Annual Return:	9% (1975–1999)
Worst 25-Year Annual Return:	6% (1955–1979)
Value of $1 after Best 25 Years:	$9
Value of $1 after Worst 25 Years:	$4

IFA "Bright Red" Portfolio (Most Aggressive)

Asset Mix: 0% bonds, 64% U.S. stocks, 18% international stocks, 6% emerging markets stocks, 5% REITs

Period: 1956–2005

Average Annualized Return:	14%	
Risk (Standard Deviation):	19%	(S&P 500 is 20%)
Best 1-Year Annual Return:	69%	(2003–2004)
Worst 1-Year Annual Return:	–35%	(1973–1974)
Best 5-Year Annual Return:	33%	(1982–1987)
Worst 5-Year Annual Return:	–4%	(1969–1974)
Best 25-Year Annual Return:	19%	(1975–1999)
Worst 25-Year Annual Return:	12%	(1955–1980)
Value of $1 after Best 25 Years:	$83	
Value of $1 after Worst 25 Years:	$18	

This is what diversification does. Note that the average long-term returns for the two portfolios range from only 7% to 14%. Note that this seemingly tight range produces a vast difference in future wealth. Note that, to achieve the higher return, you would have had to withstand far greater volatility, including a year in which your account value dropped by more than a third (and a two-year period, not shown, in which it dropped by close to half). In hindsight, hanging on through such periods seems simple ("I'm a long-term investor"). At the time, however, it would have been agonizing. After two years of brutal losses, your friends would have been fleeing the market in droves, once-bullish analysts would have been forecasting perennial gloom, and the media would have been painting Wall Street as a den of thieves. You might have blamed IFA for your losses and wanted to switch firms. You might have worried that, if you didn't yank your money out, you would lose everything. . .

Contrast this with the conservative portfolio. The worst annual decline would have been 2%, and there would have been no 5-year period in which you made less than 3% per year. Of course, after tax, the average long-term return would barely have offset inflation. In the late 1990s, moreover, when the "Bright Red" portfolio was racking up 20%-plus annual gains (and your tech-stuffed friends were bragging about their 50%-plus returns), you would have felt frustrated. You might have been annoyed at IFA for sticking you in an ossified strategy, and you might have considered ditching the firm for one that understood the "New Economy." By the end of 1999, after watching the NASDAQ nearly double in twelve months, you might have thought, "Enough." And, if you had acted on this impulse, you might have lost your shirt.

Don't Just Diversify Once:
Re-balance (but Rarely)

Maintaining adequate diversification is an ongoing process. As markets move, asset allocations within your portfolio will shift: Asset classes that have done well will grow, and those classes that have done poorly will shrink. When the shifts are significant, the risk/return profile of your portfolio will change, often undesirably. To maintain the appropriate risk/return profile, you should re-balance your portfolio occasionally (usually, once a year or once every two years).

Re-balancing is critical for three reasons. First, it allows you to maintain an appropriate risk/return profile. Second, it allows you to control your own worst instincts, which will be to invest new money in the asset classes that have recently performed the *best*. Third, it allows you to generate a higher expected return from each new investment dollar (with mean-reverting asset classes, below-average past returns eventually lead to above-average future returns). Nothing makes an investment opportunity seem more attractive than amazing past returns: If you are like most people, you will want to ditch what hasn't been working and buy more of what has been. Unfortunately, thanks to the tendency for asset classes to (eventually) regress to means, this is a recipe for disaster.

Conclusion

Diversification works—if you stick to it.

The Only Part of Your
Return You Can Control

There is only part of your return that you can *directly* control: costs. So don't be like the average boob, who ignores them.

The portfolio returns in the previous chapter are presented after fees and costs, which is admirable. Some advisors don't include fees in performance charts—for obvious reasons. High costs can obliterate your returns. Even low ones can seriously dent them.

The four big categories of costs are:

- Transaction costs
- Management and advisory fees
- Taxes
- Inflation

We've dealt with the horrors of inflation. For the sake of your self-defense skills, however, we need to spend more time on the others.

Transaction Costs

Most past returns, including the 10% average U.S. equity return, are market returns. Unfortunately, you can't buy "markets." All you can buy are securities and funds. And when you buy (or sell) securities and funds, you pay transaction costs.

If you buy stocks and bonds, your transaction costs are primarily brokerage commissions and bid-ask spreads. Commissions are usually based on a flat fee per trade or a price per share. On the bid-ask side, to buy a stock that last traded at $10, you might have to pay $10.25, and to sell the same stock, you might have to accept $9.75. This difference between the quoted price and your realized price can end up costing you more than the commission. Based on a study of discount-brokerage customers, professors Brad Barber and Terrance Odean estimate that the average round-trip trade (purchase and sale) costs 4% of value of the position. That may not sound like much, but it adds up quickly.

If you buy mutual funds instead of individual stocks and bonds, your fund pays the brokerage commissions and bid-ask spreads (with your money), but eases the pain by never mentioning them. For funds, too, however, these transaction costs can be huge—especially if the fund trades a lot. Funds pay low brokerage commissions, but they incur market-impact and timing costs that individual investors don't. A fund trying to dump a million shares of a stock might severely depress the stock's price, especially in a declining market, when there might be few buyers (as always, price is determined by the balance of supply and demand). The fund also might not be able to sell (or buy) its position rapidly, and every hour or day it takes to complete the trade might mean a lower (or higher) realized price.* Most funds generate significant transaction costs, even if you don't know they're there. But rest assured—you're paying for them.

If you just can't bring yourself to care about see-no-evil transaction costs, bear in mind that some funds charge a transaction fee, or "load," when you buy or sell the funds themselves** Loads are less common than they used to be (because fund customers have wised up), but they still exist. Imagine a car dealer saying, "Well, the car costs $25,000, but if you want to buy it, you also have to pay me $2,000." Loads only exist because some fund buyers have no clue what they are buying. Never buy funds with loads. If your broker tries to sell you one, give him the silent treatment.

Your total transaction costs will depend on the number of transactions you make and the efficiency with which you make them. In aggregate, though, even before loads, transaction costs can eat up to 1.0% of your assets per year.

---

*If the fund started buying a stock at $10, for example, its buying might drive the price up. In a rising market, in the time it took the fund to accumulate, say, a million shares, the stock's price might have risen to $11 or even $12 per share. The fund's average buy-price, therefore, would not be the $10 at which it initiated the trade, but the $11ish average. If the fund later sold the stock at, say, $15, this market impact and market timing difference would consume a healthy chunk of the return.

**Loads are not the same as early redemption fees, which are designed to deter frequent fund trading. Many funds, sensibly, ask investors to commit for a year or two, so the portfolio manager has more flexibility.

Management and Advisory Fees

Next come fees—fees charged by brokerage firms, investment advisors and fund managers. Fees can seem immaterial: "One or two percent a year? Who cares?" In fact, they are often debilitating.

The average mutual fund charges 1.5% of assets per year. Some charge more than 2%. Hedge funds usually grab 1%–2%, plus 20% of gains. Funds of funds, one of today's vogue products, often take 1% of assets plus 10% of gains *on top of* the underlying hedge fund fees, resulting in total fees of 3% or more. Some mutual funds layer on so-called 12b–1 fees, which are used to pay marketing and distribution costs and, sometimes, your broker. The car-dealer analogy for this latter gouge would be, "The car costs $25,000—plus $500 a year for my commission and our next Superbowl ad." 12b–1 fees are as offensive as loads. Never buy funds that charge them.

Management and advisory fees can range from a fraction of a percent of your portfolio per year to an astronomical 3% plus. One way to begin to appreciate their impact is to translate percentages into standard price tags. For example, a 1% annual fee means $1,000 a year for every $100,000. Even this dollar translation, however, vastly understates the total cost. The real cost will not be the fees themselves, but the loss of the *compounded* value of the fees.

Many investors don't even know what fees they are paying, much less care. To get passionate, all you have to do is run the long-term numbers. Let's return to our hypothetical $100,000 account. Let's assume that the gross return (pre-costs) is 10% and you pay 1.5% in fees. (Bear in mind that the resulting net returns are still *pretax*—you aren't finished paying your investing bills by a long shot.)

Initial Investment: $100,000
Gross Return (Pre-Fees): 10%
Annual Fees: 1.5%

Returns After:	10 Years	25 Years	50 Years
Gross:	$259,000	$1,083,000	$11,739,000
Net:	$223,000	$743,000	$5,513,000
Total Cost:	$36,000	$341,000	$6,225,000
Fees Paid:	$24,000	$127,000	$1,070,000
Add'l Lost Gain*:	$12,000	$213,000	$5,156,000

In other words, advisory fees create two kinds of "costs." The first is the actual amount you pay your advisors—the dollars they scoop out of your account every year. The second and far larger cost, however, is the amount you *would have earned* had the fees still been compounding in your account. At a 10% rate of return, every dollar you save and invest today will be worth $117 in fifty years. If you no longer have the dollar, however—if you have paid it to an advisor or fund manager—it will be worth exactly zero (to you).

These are not pie-in-the-sky scenarios. If you are under forty, chances are good that you or your spouse will have an investment horizon that approaches fifty years. If you invest

---

*The compounded amount you would have earned from the fees if you had not paid them. This does not include the fees themselves.

$100,000 today at a gross return of 10% with no costs, you should have $12 million in fifty years. If you invest the same $100,000 and pay just 1.5% in annual costs, you will have *less than half as much*. That "immaterial" 1.5%, in other words, will cost you $6.2 million. Now do you care?

Taxes

Next, we come to the biggest expense of all: taxes. Except in retirement accounts, investment gains, interest and dividends are taxed. Most advisors don't show you *after-tax* returns, and most mutual funds don't care about after-tax returns (because most investors don't). This is too bad, because the only returns that matter are after-tax, and taxes can chew off 40% or more of your pretax gains.

The silver lining of a very dark cloud is that, as with advisory fees, you have some control. Your taxes depend on your circumstances (tax bracket, state of residence, etc.), and they also depend on your advisors' tax efficiency and the type of account in which your assets are held. You can choose advisors and managers who focus on after-tax returns, and you can control where you hold your assets.

The key is to recognize that pretax returns are not created equal. A typical active fund buys and sells stocks so often that it generates lots of short-term capital gains, which are taxed at high rates. A well-managed passive fund, meanwhile, generates mostly long-term capital gains, which are taxed at lower rates. For taxable investors, therefore, the passive fund is almost always a better choice. A *tax-managed* fund goes even further, avoiding dividend income and offsetting losses against gains. Before you make any investment decisions, you should view your entire financial life from an after-tax perspective, making choices with an eye toward maximizing *your* return instead of Uncle Sam's.

How much can tax-related decisions affect your returns? Thanks to interest-exemption, a 5% yield on triple-tax-exempt municipal bonds can be worth more than an 8.5% yield on corporate bonds. Thanks to short-term versus long-term capital gains, a 5% return on an index fund can be worth more than a 7% return on an actively managed stock fund. As shown below, the same 8.5% pretax return on a stock fund can produce very different after-tax returns, depending on what percentage comes from short-term gains versus dividends and long-term gains:

Impact of Fund Turnover on After-Tax Returns

Investment:	$100,000
Net Pretax Return:	8.5%
Income Tax Bracket:	40%
LT Cap Gains Tax:	15%
High-Turnover Fund	
Net Pretax Return:	$8,500
% Short-Term Gains:	100%
Taxes:	$3,400
Net After-Tax Return $:	$5,100
Net After-Tax Return %:	5.1%
Low-Turnover Fund	
Net Pretax Return $:	$8,500

% Short-Term Gains:	0%
Taxes:	$1,275
Net After-Tax Return $:	$7,225
Net After-Tax Return %:	7.2%

As with advisory fees, every dollar you save on taxes compounds in your account. Your long-term savings, therefore, end up being far greater than what you didn't pay in taxes. $100,000 invested at 5% for fifty years compounds to just north of $1 million. The same $100,000 invested at 7% compounds to $3 million. Tax efficiency matters. A lot.

Inflation

Lastly, we return to inflation. Inflation isn't an explicit cost, but it might as well be. Depending on the era, inflation usually ranges between 2% and 6%. Unlike the costs above, you "pay" for inflation regardless of what you invest in. With inflation, you are helpless. You can't run, you can't hide. You can't blame your financial advisor; you can only sob on his or her shoulder as your money drains away. All you can do about inflation is reduce the damage by investing some of your portfolio in asset classes that, over the long run, weather inflation, such as TIPS, REITs and stocks.

Conclusion

If you don't pay attention, fees and taxes will gobble as much as 5% of your portfolio each year, and inflation will likely wipe out another 3%. This might be okay if your advisors could generate 30% gains every year, but they almost certainly can't. Over the long haul, these costs can destroy your returns.

Never make a move without first analyzing costs. Never transact when you don't have to. Never pay higher fees than you have to. Never ignore the impact of taxes. And never forget that inflation means you're making a lot less than you think.

A Self-Defense Preparedness Quiz

Congratulations! You should now have a solid foundation for practicing Wall Street self-defense. Before you start using it, however, you need to ask yourself some questions.

First and foremost, you need to figure out what you want to accomplish. For example, are you saving for retirement, college tuitions or a new house? Are you trying to shoot the moon, or just gradually increase your nest egg? The answers to these questions should affect every decision you make, from whether you hire an advisor, to what asset allocation mix you choose, to how much you pay for investment services. The only reason to make any investment decision is to try to accomplish something. Before you do anything else, therefore, you need to decide what that is.

Second, you need to be honest with yourself about your risk tolerance. Specifically, you need to imagine how you would feel if your portfolio fell by, say, 10%, 25% or 50% in a year. Why? Because this will also affect your asset allocation decisions. If you choose an aggressive strategy, your portfolio could get cut in half even if you do everything right. If you can't stomach such a plunge, you need to know in advance, or you will likely panic and sell at the bottom—a devastating mistake. If you select a strategy that is too conservative, meanwhile, you might cheat yourself of potential return.

Third, you need to figure out your investment time horizon. This, too, should affect your asset allocation decisions. The longer your time horizon, the more you can ignore near-term volatility, and the more aggressively you can structure your portfolio.

Fourth, you need to be honest about how much time you want to devote to managing your money. If the answer is "none," you have two choices: Hire a full-service financial advisor, or buy a low-cost, globally diversified "life cycle" fund, which will change its target asset allocation (and, therefore, risk) as you age. If your answer is "a little," you can learn the basics of diversification and cost control, implement them with low-cost funds, and then re-balance your portfolio every once in a while. This might—*might*—allow you to do slightly better than a life cycle fund. If your answer is "several hours a week," you are in extreme danger, whether or not you hire an advisor. Your extra effort, combined with your advisor's enthusiasm for your trading habit, will lead to overconfidence, and you will likely trade too much. If your answer is "all my time," you should just go into the money management business.

Fifth, you need to understand what your advisors can know and control and what they can't know and control—and you need to try not to blame them for the latter, unless they pretend (or think) they can control it. Many investors evaluate their advisor's performance by how much their accounts go up or down. Unfortunately, in most cases, this is unfair: Advisors can't control or predict what will happen to your account over the next few months or years, and what does happen tells you little about their competence. (This often works to an advisor's advantage, of course: If the market goes up, you will tend to think your advisor is brilliant, even if he's an idiot.) Few investors, meanwhile, evaluate advisors based on factors they can and should control: Asset allocation, diversification, cost reduction, risk assessment, tax management, expectations management, expertise and commitment. If you think it's frustrating to hire an advisor only to lose money, imagine how an advisor feels after getting fired because the market dropped.

Once you figure out the honest answers to all these questions, *write them down*. Doing so will give you a snapshot of your current thinking and help you decide what to do. It will enable you to give specific guidelines to any advisors you hire (and hold their feet to the fire should they deviate from your plan). Just as important, it will help you *stick* to your plan, whenever the forces of boredom, fear, peer pressure, inertia, envy and greed intervene. On the negative side, writing the answers down will make it harder to blame someone else for everything that goes wrong. We love to take credit for success and blame others for failure, and putting your plan in writing will make it harder to avoid responsibility. (Of course, you can always rip the paper up.)

Finally, before we charge into the fray, as a basic assessment of your self-defense skills, answer the following true/false questions. (For the fun of it, answer them right now—just put a T or F in the margin.) *Be honest.*

1. One of my investing goals is to challenge myself and have fun.
2. I know most investors can't beat the market over the long term, but I think I can.
3. I can control my return by buying the right mix of stocks and bonds.
4. If I buy a dozen stocks, I'll be diversified.

5. Which stocks I buy is more important than how much I allocate to "stocks."
6. A percentage point or two of fees doesn't matter.
7. I don't really care how good my return is; I just want an advisor I like.
8. A good advisor will get me out before a crash.
9. I don't know enough to manage my own money.
10. I expect that the pretax, long-term, annual return for my portfolio will be (mark one of the following "True"):
   - Less than 7%
   - Between 7% and 14%
   - Between 14% and 21.5%
   - More than 21.5%

What is important here is that you be honest. This said, if you answered TRUE to more than Question 10, your command of the facts and, therefore, your odds of practicing effective self-defense, are low. (For your own sake, I would strongly suggest re-reading this section of the book or a few of the foundation books cited in the Further Reading list.) If, meanwhile, you answered FALSE to all but the last question, your odds are good.

In case you're interested, here's why the answers should be FALSE:

1. *One of my investing goals is to challenge myself and have fun.* Then you haven't drawn a distinction between investing and entertainment. To understand why you *must* do this, see Chapter 2. To learn how to challenge yourself, have fun, *and* clearly distinguish between investing and entertainment, read on.

2. *I know most investors can't beat the market, but I think I can.* Why? Because most investors are stupid? Because you are a genius? Because you picked some winners last year? Because you have a smart advisor? Because you subscribe to nine market newsletters? Because you've outperformed the market for two years? Because you have inside information? If you don't know the answer—and if it's not a really good answer—you are kidding yourself. See Chapters six, seven, eight and nine.

3. *I can control my return by buying the right mix of stocks and bonds.* Unfortunately, you can't. You can control your *risk* and *expected return* by buying a diversified mix of stocks and bonds, but your gross return will always be determined by forces you can't control (market performance). The good news is you *can* control one part of your return: your costs. So devote a lot of your energy to keeping them as low as possible.

4. *If I buy a dozen stocks, I'll be diversified enough.* Not unless your idea of "acceptable risk" is driving 120 miles per hour at night with the headlights off. If you buy a dozen stocks from different industries you will be modestly diversified within a single, risky asset class. If you buy a dozen stocks from the same industry group, you will barely be diversified at all. If you have an average risk profile, you should probably own stocks (or, better yet, funds) from the United States, international and emerging markets, as well as some bonds and REITs. See Chapter Ten.

5. *Which stocks I buy is more important than how much I allocate to "stocks."* No, it isn't. Assuming you are well-diversified,

the biggest contributor to your return will be the amount you have allocated to the underlying asset classes, not which stocks or bonds you buy.

6. *A percentage point or two of fees is meaningless.* Unfortunately, it isn't. A 1.5% fee will likely cost you more than half of your potential gain over the next fifty years.

7. *I don't really care how good my return is; I just want an advisor I like.* Then you are aiming pretty low, considering that your standard of living for the last third of your life may depend on your return. There are plenty of trustworthy and competent advisors out there—assuming you really need one.

8. *A good advisor will get me out of the market before a crash.* Not without missing some major market booms in the process (and setting you up for taxes, costs and disappointment galore). If crashes were predictable, everyone would get out ahead of them.

9. *I don't know enough to manage my money myself.* Actually, if you've read this far, you do. All you really need to know is that returns are a function of risk, appropriate diversification and cost control and that all are easily achieved in a low-cost, passively managed life cycle fund. What you probably do not know enough to do— almost no one does—is pick stocks well enough to consistently beat the market.

10. *I expect that the net, pretax, long-term return* for my portfolio will be:*

---

*After transaction costs and advisory fees, but before taxes and inflation.

- *Less than 7%.* If so, you are a well-informed realist, and thus have a chance of bumping your return into the next category.

- *Between 7% and 14%.* If so, you expect a return between that of the "most conservative" and "most aggressive" portfolios in Chapter Ten. The low end of this range is a reasonable expectation—if your time horizon is long enough, if you control costs and if you don't make mistakes.

- *Between 14% and 21.5%.* You are expecting to do about as well as David Swensen, Yale University's renowned endowment manager, who has access to the best funds, information and expertise in the world. His long-term return is 16%.

- *More than 21.5%.* You are expecting to do better than Warren Buffett, the most legendary investor in history. (Well, okay, that's his after-tax return, but still. . .)

PART 2
PRACTICING SELF-DEFENSE

Investment Advisors

Meet Your Investment Advisor

A few years ago, I participated in one of the most iconic of Wall Street rituals: a meeting with an investment advisor. Why? For the same reason most people do: I wanted advice. The advisor I met with worked at a full-service Wall Street brokerage firm in a leather-trimmed office in a Manhattan sky-scraper. He was a chipper thirty-something, full of ideas, opinions and confidence.

At the advisor's suggestion, I had previously submitted financial details—assets, risk tolerance, time horizon, objectives, etc.—so he could develop a proposed investment program. Having vaporized a chunk of my portfolio in the market crash, I had one main objective: To avoid losing money. Having also vaporized my immediate employment prospects, I had a secondary objective: To generate some income.

As is customary in such meetings, the advisor showed me into a luxurious conference room. He then handed me a gorgeous presentation book and skipped to the punch line:

With careful asset allocation, manager selection and portfolio rebalancing, we could generate low-risk returns of about 10% per year.

Ten percent a year? A decade earlier, in the 1990s boom, this would have prompted a yawn. Now, after a two-year bear market, it sounded marvelous—especially the low-risk part. We burrowed into the presentation book.

The good news: Most of the advice inside was responsible and sane. The proposed program emphasized asset allocation (instead of stock picking), diversification (instead of swinging for fences) and patience (instead of trying to predict short-term performance). The program was personalized (if yours isn't, head for the elevators). It didn't tout the advisor's prowess as a stock picking wizard (if yours does, sprint for the elevators). It didn't extol the brilliance of the firm's analysts and economists. It didn't promise market-beating returns. It didn't offer to help me find the "next Microsoft." It illustrated that the projected return was only a median, that the actual return might be as much as six percentage points higher or lower (responsible financial projections are more akin to sawed-off shotgun blasts than laser beams). It disclosed all fees, in both percentage and dollar terms.

The presentation, in other words, got the most important stuff right. As the advisor suggested, the proposed program would probably make me a little money without much risk. What it would not do, I thought, was generate anything like a 10% average return (in the presentation book, the projected return was 9%—the advisor had rounded up—but this, too, seemed a stretch).

When gazing at a presentation book filled with beautiful pie charts, graphs and tables created just for you, it is easy to

Five Questions to Ask a
Prospective Investment Advisor

As you narrow down your search, ask prospective advisors tons of questions, including ones you know the answers to. If you ever feel uncomfortable—or get the sense that the advisors are being less than straightforward—eliminate them. Try to ask questions that reveal what kind of people they are, as well as how they approach their craft. Here are some good ones (and some good answers):

1. *Why have clients left you?* An ideal answer would be, "Some of my clients kept wanting to try to beat the market, and I just don't think that's a wise strategy."

2. *What do you think of indexing as an investment strategy?* If the advisor thinks indexing "guarantees mediocrity," he doesn't know his facts.

3. *What do you see as your primary responsibility?* Best-case scenario: "To develop and implement an investment program tailored to your needs and circumstances and then help you stick with it."

4. *How do you predict a mutual fund's future performance?* The best measure is the fund's expense ratio—not Lipper/Morningstar ratings, past performance, fund family or manager tenure.

5. *What do you think the market is going to do?* Something along the lines of, "Over the short term, I don't know. I would respectfully suggest, however, that no one else does, either. Over the long term, I expect the market to deliver something close to a 10% return. My goal is to help you design and implement a strategy with an appropriate expected risk-adjusted return regardless of what the market does."

forget that projected returns are just black marks on a page. Far more important are the assumptions and logic underlying them. As I flipped through the book, I searched for the "Assumptions" page. And that's where the bad news began: There was no "Assumptions" page.

I asked the advisor how the projected returns had been calculated. He didn't know (uh oh). He also didn't know, at first, whether the projected returns were before fees and transaction costs—or after. He soon determined, not surprisingly, that they were before costs, and, just like that, the 9% return dropped to about 7%. The projected returns were also shown before taxes and inflation, which meant that, even if I believed the gross projections—which, after scrutiny, I didn't—the *net, after-tax, real* projected return was about 2%. It would be nice to expect to see fully adjusted returns (after fees, taxes and inflation) in a sales presentation, but, unfortunately, this is fantasy.

The advisor didn't know how the projected returns had been calculated. He also didn't know how the firm had chosen its outside managers (other than typical blather about "rigorous selection process," "careful scrutiny," etc.). He acknowledged that the fees on the firm's fund-of-funds hedge fund product were hefty, and that the rate of interest the firm paid on cash was half a point lower than at low-cost firms like Vanguard. To his credit, the advisor did not try to argue that his firm's cash accounts were still "better." He dropped the name of a client—which worried me, because I assumed that he would not hesitate to drop mine. He recognized quickly that I was focused on costs, and then suggested ways we could reduce them.

Despite some concerns, the presentation seemed sound, and compared to some of what passes for quality investment advice, it was. Knowing the importance of costs, I still sent most of my savings to Vanguard (a smart decision). Fearing a market crash, I did not follow the advisor's recommendation to increase my equity allocation, and I kept most of my portfolio in cash (a dumb decision). I also decided to implement one of the advisor's recommendations: I hired the firm to build me a portfolio of tax-exempt municipal bonds (a mediocre decision, given the cost).

So, overall, how did I do in terms of Wall Street self-defense? Fine, not great. In hindsight, I would give myself a "B."

I didn't forget what the meeting was (a sales pitch) or what the advisor's job was (to sell me products). I didn't forget what *my* job was (to evaluate the products, including the advisor). I scrutinized costs. I didn't put much faith in the projected returns. I didn't assume that the advisor's manager-selection process would enable him to pick managers who would beat the market. I didn't plunge into outrageously priced "alternative investment" products just because hedge funds were all the rage. I didn't assume that, because the advisor was eager to hold forth on the market, he knew what it was going to do.

This said, I should have been more demanding. I paid too much for a plain-vanilla bond ladder, and I didn't focus on the fact that the firm was not obligated to construct it exactly the way I wanted.* I also didn't heed clues that discretion and confidentiality weren't at the top of the advisor's priority list. In hindsight, therefore, it should have come as no surprise that the firm's bond ladder locked me into low interest rates

---

*I wanted short-term maturities—bonds that mature within two to three years. I got mostly long-term maturities—bonds that mature in 5–10 years.

for a decade or that information I assumed was confidential would later appear in a book written by one of my advisor's friends.

To Hire or Not to Hire (an Investment Advisor)?

The first question on the subject of investment advisors is whether to hire one. Given the vast array of do-it-yourself resources out there, from discount brokerage firms to fund supermarkets, to one-decision (really) life cycle funds, to low-cost financial plans offered by firms like Vanguard, T. Rowe Price, and Fidelity, it is reasonable—and, in many cases, smart—to go it alone.

I have poked some fun at advisors in past chapters, so let me start this one by paying (some of) them a compliment. Over the course of your lifetime, a competent advisor could, literally, be worth her weight in gold.*

Such an advisor will help you figure out how much money you need to save—as well as how to save it. She will allocate your assets appropriately and keep your costs low, a strategy that will make less money for her but more for you. She will focus on what can be known and controlled (and explain why) and help you ignore what can't be known or controlled. She will help you develop *and stick with* a long-term strategy. She might increase your allocation to stocks after a bear market, when less-competent advisors would decrease it, and

---

*Approximately $1,280,000, assuming your advisor weighs 160 pounds and gold sells for $500 an ounce. To save (or earn) you this much, the advisor would have to generate a 4% annual return after fees on a $500,000 portfolio for twenty-five years above and beyond what you would have earned on your own.

reduce your exposure after a bull market, when less-competent advisors would increase it. She will keep your money out of sectors and stocks du jour, despite your pleas, and she will do this deftly enough so as not to get fired. She will focus on *real, after-tax, after-cost* returns, not the irrelevant pretax, gross performance that lesser advisors pat themselves on the back for.

In addition, a talented advisor might offer expertise on estate planning, insurance, mortgages, tax or banking services. She might buy you dinner occasionally, or get you U.S. Open tickets. (This used to be my advisor's specialty. When I was a big-shot, I got passes to an air-conditioned suite in Arthur Ashe Stadium with a television and cheese plates. The next year, as I was falling from grace—like a stone—I got a seat so far up that I had to watch the match on the stadium TV screen. Since switching to Vanguard, of course, I have watched the Open from my kitchen table.) Above all, a talented advisor can dissuade you from being stupid—an invaluable service, one we can all benefit from.

If your advisor does all these jobs well, she will have a chance of paying for herself over the long term (only a chance, unfortunately), at least relative to the performance of a low-cost life cycle fund. And if she does them really well, hiring her will be one of the best investment decisions of your life.

Lest this uplifting commercial tempt you to rush out and hire an advisor, however, here's the fine print: Many advisors are, um, not competent, and if you hand your money to a bozo, you can kiss a plush retirement goodbye. Worse, you can't protect yourself from this fate simply by avoiding self-evident morons. The most dangerous advisors are the ones who are charming, articulate, persuasive, successful, trustworthy—and incompetent.

In any case, before worrying about how to find a high-quality advisor, you should decide whether you really need one. There are a few valid reasons to hire a full-service investment advisor, and many bogus ones. Here are some of the valid ones:

Valid Reasons to Hire a Financial Advisor

- *You want true investment expertise, and you are confident that you can find an advisor who has it.* Thankfully, some advisors do have it. Most, unfortunately, don't. Another problem: You stand a better chance of finding a real expert if you are already rich. The advisory business is a high-fixed cost, low-variable cost business, so advisors make more money managing big accounts than small ones. Thus, talent in the advisory business tends to migrate up. Talented advisors often establish minimum account sizes of $2 million or more. Just as important, the quality of basic advice offered by broker-less fund firms like Vanguard and Fidelity is often excellent, and it is also usually a heck of a lot cheaper than a full-service advisor.
- *You know nothing about investing, don't want to learn and don't trust a voice on a telephone.* Fine. But remember that even dedicated advisors are mostly just a voice on a telephone, so don't go overboard about the importance of a "personal relationship."
- *You want someone to talk to.*
- *You want to get schmoozed.*
- *You require esoteric planning or tax skills.*
- *You want someone to "just take care of everything."* Given how tedious many people find financial matters, this is understandable. It is also, however, extremely danger-

ous. If you hire the wrong advisor to "just take care of everything," you may eventually find yourself taking care of little or nothing.

- *You already have an advisor you trust, and don't want to fire him or her.*
- *You want access to products and services you can't get on your own.*
- *You are so rich that you don't care about costs.*
- *You want someone to blame.*

Any advisor worth his or her salt will expound on these reasons and more, so we don't need to spend time on them. Since the same would-be advisors will also probably offer a dozen *bogus* reasons why you should hire them, however, it's worth listing a few of those, too:

Bogus Reasons to Hire a Financial Advisor

- *Index funds just guarantee mediocrity.* Wrong. Any advisor who says this doesn't know what he is talking about (or worse).
- *Of course you can beat the market—just look at Warren Buffett.* The issue is not whether Warren Buffett can beat the market. It's whether it's in your best interests to try. In most cases, it isn't, and a good advisor should know this.
- *Our rigorous selection process will find the funds that beat the market.* Really? Is the advisor willing to guarantee that? Will he waive all fees in periods in which his chosen funds don't beat the market? Will he make up for lost returns?
- *We'll get you out before a crash.* Great! And will he refund your losses if he doesn't?

- *We'll get you into the next Microsoft.* How?
- *Our analysts and strategists are the smartest in the business.* Almost certainly not true. Also, beside the point. IQ doesn't necessarily translate into above-market returns.
- *Higher fees mean higher skill: You get what you pay for.* Wrong. In fact, in most cases, the less you pay, the better you are likely to do, because every dollar of fees reduces your returns.
- *Our clients have beaten the market for the past three years.* What does he mean by "market"—the S&P 500? If so, big whoop. Most small-stock and value-stock funds have beaten the market in the last three years (at this writing). And, by the way, is that after costs and fees? Taxes? Have *all* the advisor's clients beaten the market, or just the ones who happened to buy small-cap and value stocks? Did the advisor recommend these stocks/funds, or did the clients already own them? Why did he recommend them? What kinds of funds will out-perform next? Does he think he can time the market? Will he guarantee your losses if he doesn't?
- *Vanguard can't get you stock in hot IPOs.** True. But you probably shouldn't be buying IPOs. And how many shares of each hot IPO will the advisor get you, anyway? Enough to cover his annual fees? What if the "hot IPO" turns out to be a bust?
- *Your retirement fund is too important to manage yourself.* Possibly true. But this doesn't mean the advisor will be any better at it.

---

*IPO = Initial Public Offering. In hot markets, everyone wants some of these. Why? Because they are intentionally underpriced. So those who get shares at the offering price get the closest a speculator ever gets to a sure thing.

- *Our fees are only 1.25% per year.* Even 1.25% per year takes a huge bite out of returns.

Advisors have an advantage when dispensing this bunk, because they will be telling you what you want to hear: "Index funds are for losers!" "I can beat the market!" "I'll pick the next Microsoft!" As always, be honest with yourself: If you hire an advisor for one of these reasons, you're making a mistake.

And here, meanwhile, are some valid reasons *not* to hire a full-service financial advisor:

Valid Reasons NOT to Hire a Financial Advisor

- Cost
- The potential for well-disguised incompetence
- The potential for an expensive, painful divorce
- The availability of competent, low-priced and personalized financial advice

No matter what would-be advisors say, the biggest reason not to hire one is cost. Most advisors charge between 0.5% and 1.5% of assets per year. This may not sound like much, and, from the advisor's perspective, it often isn't.* From your perspective, however, it's a boatload.

Many advisors, moreover, will charge you an advisory fee and then buy you garden-variety funds or stocks that result in *additional* management and transaction fees. If your advisor

---

*An investment advisory firm paid 1% of assets must manage $100 million to generate $1 million a year in revenue. After administration, research, compliance, legal, training, information and other costs, this doesn't leave all that much for the actual advisors to take home.

charges 1% and buys funds that charge 1%, your total fee load will be 2%. On a $100,000 investment, a 2% fee will cost you $7.5 million over fifty years—two-thirds of your $12 million no-cost return. Pay total fees of 2.5% for fifty years and you can kiss $8.5 million of your potential $12 million goodbye.

Over shorter time horizons, fees hurt less, but they are still significant. In twenty-five years, $100,000 compounding at 10% will grow to $1.1 million with no fees. A 1.5% fee, meanwhile, will eat almost a third of this ($341,000) and a 2.5% fee about half ($508,000). In other words, if you plan to retire on $100,000 invested for twenty-five years, you had better make sure you're factoring in fees.

So when assessing whether or not to hire a financial advisor, recognize that the cost of employing one is high. To justify a 1% fee on your $100,000 account, your advisor will have to add more than $4.6 million of value over the next fifty years. To do this, he or she will have to boost your *net* return by approximately 1.25% per year, which will mean boosting your gross return by 2.25%. Although this may sound easy, it can be a tall order if the alternatives to an advisor are efficient, low-cost life cycle or index funds.* (If the alternative is day-trading, an advisor will probably pay for herself ten times over.)

Let's look at a real-world example. At this writing, the Vanguard Target Retirement 2035 Fund, a low-cost life cycle fund composed of U.S. stocks, international stocks and U.S. bonds, charges an annual fee of 0.21%. The average advisor

---

*To put this in context, the average mutual fund manager beats the market by 1% *on a gross basis*. Therefore, if your advisor does as well as the average mutual fund manager—a professional stock picker whose only job is stock picking—he still won't cover his cost.

might charge about 1.5%, all in (i.e., including fund fees, brokerage fees, etc.). Assuming a 10% gross return, $100,000 in the Vanguard fund would grow to about $1 million over twenty-five years. On the advisor's watch, meanwhile, the same investment would grow to about $750,000. Although the advisor will surely believe he will add enough value to more than offset this (a gross return of 12.5% or better), he probably won't. This is especially true if the account in question is a retirement account. (Advisors can add real value in tax-management, but retirement accounts grow tax free.)

The ultimate pitch from most advisors, of course, will be "You can't afford *not* to hire an advisor." Again, if the alternative is day-trading or a savings account, this might be true. If, however, you are comfortable enough with the concepts of diversification, asset allocation, and indexing to buy a life cycle fund, you absolutely *can* afford not to. In fact, unless you really want your hand held—or are confident that you have found a superior advisory firm—you should probably forgo a full-service advisor and invest through a low-cost fund firm. The caveat is that, if you choose this route, you need to be confident in your ability to withstand severe bear markets. It is easy to be a do-it-yourselfer when prices are going up. It is harder when you're getting slammed. One of the most valuable services a (talented) advisor can provide is reassurance in tough times, and if this reassurance helps you stick to a plan you otherwise would have aborted, the fees will have been worth it.

Meanwhile, if you're uncomfortable making your own decisions, if you want someone to help you keep your financial house in order, or if you are confident you have found a superior advisory firm, then it's worth hiring an advisor. Just be careful who you choose and how much you pay.

What Investment Advisors Are Selling These Days

To strengthen your investment advisor self-defense skills, it helps to know what they are likely to try to sell you. To get an up-to-date sense of this, I recently reviewed a lot of advice. (A friend who met with more than a dozen firms was kind enough to send me their materials in a fifty-pound box.) Specifically, I have reviewed advice from major brokerage firms, regional brokerage firms, discount brokerage firms, independent advisory firms, independent money managers, mutual fund firms and massive financial conglomerates.

This research has revealed some good news about the state of the advisory business—and some bad news. Before we get to that, though, here's a summary of what investment advisors are selling these days:

- *A Disciplined Investment Process*: The cornerstone of any sound investment program. Also so basic that it's like a car company promising that your new sedan will have four wheels.
- *Personalized Investment Solutions*: Just a fancy way of saying "advice," but ditto. Personalized advice, by the way, is what distinguishes an investment advisor from a mere commentator or pundit.
- *Experience*: Helpful as long as it's money management experience and not just asset-gathering, product-selling and client-pacifying experience. If your prospective advisors don't show evidence of having learned from and

been humbled by their asset-management experiences, look out.

- *Trust*: Critical. Unfortunately, also relative. You need to trust your advisor to do well by you. Your advisor's family and bosses, meanwhile, need to trust the advisor to do well by *them*. This divides your advisor's loyalties even if he or she is the most trustworthy person in the world.

- *Uniqueness*: There are important differences between advisory firms, but they are often hard to pinpoint and evaluate. For example: methodology (Does their method work? How do they know? Has it been independently tested?), discipline (Do they stick to it?), intellectual rigor (Are they driven by a desire to get it right or just win your business?), integrity (When they don't know, do they say so?), products (Truly different, or just generic?), and prices (High? Low? Exorbitant?). The difference is in the details, and to distract you many firms just bury you in fluffy clichés, selective data and primo tee times.

- *Appropriate Asset Allocation*: Thankfully, Wall Street has largely stopped selling stock picking, industry-picking, and market-timing advice: Only a few firms still suggest they can pick winners and get you in or out ahead of the crowd. Instead, most of Wall Street wisely recommends that you divide your portfolio among asset classes to achieve the optimal mix of risk and return. This is great news.

- *Manager Selection*: Alas, even as Wall Street has stopped selling stock picking, it is now hyping another dubious practice: Manager picking. Almost every firm devotes multiple pages to its manager selection process, in which it screens 20,000-plus money managers and selects the few worthy of managing your money. The chosen managers, not surprisingly, have excellent past performance. The presentations note that "past performance is not indicative of future results," but such performance is still offered as proof of the chosen managers' talent. In other words, the firms either believe that past performance *is* indicative of future results (wrong) or believe that you will (right).

- *Alpha*: Most firms sell "alpha"—the return that a skilled manager generates above the appropriate benchmark. Specifically, the firms suggest that they can identify managers who will beat the market. How? By showing you examples of managers who have delivered alpha in the past. The implication, as always, is that managers who have generated alpha in the past will generate it in the future. Unfortunately, there is little evidence that they will. There is also little evidence that any firm can consistently select managers that will deliver *future* alpha (although we can all do it in hindsight). Neither of these concerns stop advisory firms from selling their alpha-selection capabilities until the cows come home.

- *Tax-Managed Strategies*: One firm whose advice I reviewed—one—offered a stock picking strategy that might be expected to yield an above-market, after-tax return. This strategy consists of constructing a portfolio for each client that is designed to mimic an index but that takes the client's tax situation into account. One disadvantage of mutual funds (including index funds) is that they reduce tax flexibility: A fund owner's cost basis is the price of the *fund*, not the prices of the individual securities, so the investor can't easily harvest losses with which to offset capital gains. The Tax-Efficient Structured Equity (TESE) strategy, offered by U.S. Trust, allows an investor to track the index but retain control over capital gains, thus producing a higher after-tax return. So chalk one up (one) for Wall Street active management services.

- *Alternative Investments*: Many advisors now recommend a healthy dose of hedge funds, private equity funds, real estate partnerships, absolute return funds and other "alternative investments." These products sound great on paper—"They'll make you money when the stock market's dropping!"—but they should be approached with extreme caution. First, they usually come with massive costs and fees, especially after-tax. Second, they do not necessarily provide as much diversification benefit as they appear to. And, third, as with standard asset classes, the advisor's ability to select the few managers that have a strong likelihood of posting excess returns is probably less than the advisor implies.

- *Pre-Fee, Pretax, and Pre-Inflation Returns*: Read through a few advisory pitch-books and you could be forgiven for thinking that you're going to get rich. Why? Because if you didn't have to worry about fees, taxes or inflation, you *would* get rich.

- *Fees? What Fees?*: They are disclosed, in most cases, at least in fine print. However, rare is the firm that devotes a page of the main presentation to detailing fees, and rarer still is the firm that factors a full fee load into future projections. Almost nonexistent, meanwhile (at least in my survey), is the firm that includes a chart explaining that costs are the only element of return that you can control and that, all else being equal, the lower your costs, the better your return. Also non-existent is the firm bold enough to guarantee that it is so skilled at asset allocation and manager selection that you will get what you pay for. No mystery why that is.

- *Future Wealth Scenarios*: More good news (finally). Wall Street has moved away from pinpoint return projections. The few firms that do provide projections go to great lengths to say that they are not, in fact, projections, but "hypothetical scenarios," and that the scenarios represent nothing more than a range of possible returns. On the one hand, this is ridiculous: Of course they are projections. On the other hand, it's honest: The best any forecaster can do is handicap a range of possible outcomes.

- *Expertise Backed Up by Data, Facts, and Academic Research*: Thankfully, some advisory firms even sell this. As discussed, because of the economics of the advisory business, some excellent firms cater only to the super rich. But a few firms do bring the academic work to the people. The founder of a firm called Index Funds Advisors, for example, Mark Hebner, started the firm after discovering that he had sacrificed $30 million to crappy advice received from a brokerage firm. IFA invests through Dimensional Fund Advisors, a mutual-fund firm dedicated to implementing passive strategies developed by leading academics such as Eugene Fama (University of Chicago) and Kenneth French (Dartmouth). If you're a fan of stock picking, you may be annoyed by IFA's near-religious conviction that it is for the birds, but IFA knows its facts. The firm's web site (www.ifa.com) is also a treasure trove of links and data about historical market performance, passive management and other topics.*

- *Heartwarming Case Studies*: One firm provided case studies about how its team of advisors swooped in and solved intractable problems or saved helpless grannies from blowing their financial security to smithereens. Did these advisors do a good enough job to justify their humongous fees? Who knows? Who cares? By the time you finish reading the stories, you're so moved, you'll pay anything.

So that's what investment advisors are selling these days. Now here's how to protect yourself.

Caveats for the (Advisor) Emptor

1) Beware of Projected Returns

Remember the advisor I met with, the one who suggested that I would generate a low-risk return of 10% a year? Well, this was a happy claim, and I was eager to learn more about it.

The advisor's presentation book didn't have an "Assumptions" page, but later, at home, I did eventually discover a small heading called "Assumptions." And there, finally, I found what I was looking for. The assumptions, in summary, were as follows:

---

* Full disclosure: IFA's president, Mark Hebner, once bought me brunch and invited me to speak at an investment conference. He has also been a helpful source for this book.

Asset Class	Estimated Return Per Year	Recommended Allocation
3-Month T-bills	4.47%	10.0%
Municipal Bonds	7.15%	30.0%
International Stocks	4.53%	7.5%
U.S. Stocks	11.81%	37.5%
Funds of Funds	9.75%	15.0%
Total	9.1%	100.0%

This explained how I was going to generate about 10% per year with low risk: I was going to get 11.81% a year from stocks, 7.15% from municipal bonds and 4.47% from T-bills. The numbers were so precise, so reassuring: They were expressed to two decimal places! Alas, like all financial projections, they were simply black marks on a page.

Predicting market performance is not an exact science, and those who pretend it is do so at their peril. There are almost as many prediction methods as there are investors, and few are all "right" or all "wrong." (None is perfect.) That said, some methods are better than others, and this one left something to be desired.

The method the brokerage firm used—extrapolating past performance—is common. It is logical, and, in some cases, defensible. (As a tool for predicting the future, history is far from perfect, but it's all we've got.) It is also, unfortunately, dangerous. In this case, the firm's error was not that it extrapolated from history. Its error was that it didn't look at *enough* history. Specifically, it only looked at ten years, when it should have looked at fifty or more.

As previously described, in the financial markets, the "long term" is long. Over the past two hundred years, U.S. stocks have, on average, returned approximately 10% a year. For many of those two hundred years, however, stocks have returned nothing—or worse. The fallow periods, moreover, have not just lasted months or years. They have lasted decades.

The most recent market cycle spanned thirty-four years, from 1966–2000. The bull phase, the one we all remember, lasted eighteen years (1982–2000), and it took the Dow from just over 800 to just under 12,000. The bear phase—the one almost no one remembers—lasted sixteen years (sixteen years!), and it took the Dow down nearly 20%. Lest this tempt you to rush out and buy bonds, average bond returns from 1966–1981 were worse than those on stocks. (Bonds can be dangerous when inflation is rising, a fact worth remembering during this latest bear market.)

Because market cycles are so long, assumptions based on ten-year averages can lead to unfortunate conclusions. If you had applied the ten-year analysis to the S&P 500 index from 1973 to 1982, for example, you might have concluded that the index would deliver low single-digit returns over the next ten years—an outlook paltry enough for you to consider reducing your exposure to stocks. In fact, over the next ten years, the index delivered low double-digit returns. (The late 1970s and early 1980s was a great time to buy, in part because stock performance had been so crappy for so long. Of course, because of this you would have felt like a nut case for even thinking of buying.)

In 2004, meanwhile, applying the same ten-year analysis to the S&P 500 suggested that, over the next decade, the index would deliver low double-digit returns (thus the 12% assumption used by the brokerage firm). Broader history, however, suggested that the actual performance would be worse—as it had to be, if the ten-year average return was, eventually, to regress back down to the two hundred-year 10% mean.

The problem with most projections based on recent past performance is that they don't fully account for the length of market cycles and the market's tendency toward mean-regression. With this in mind, let's look again at the broker-age firm's assumptions. This time, though, let's compare the assumptions with each asset class's *long-term* return, instead of just the ten-year return.

Asset Class	10-Year Past Return	Long-Term Past Return
3-Month T-bills	4.47%	3.7%
Municipal Bonds	7.15%	4.5%
International Stocks	4.53%	10%
U.S. Stocks	11.81%	10%
Funds of Funds	9.75%	God only knows

Most of the assumptions suffer from the mean-regression problem. In 2004, interest rates were at forty-year lows. If, af-ter two decades of dropping, rates either remained where they were or, more likely, began to regress upward to the mean, bond returns would sag (because when rates rise, bond prices drop). It was hard to imagine, therefore, that municipal bonds would deliver the same returns over the next ten years as they had over the prior ten, when yields were higher and capital appreciation from falling rates juiced returns. Similarly, after two decades of above-trend U.S. stock performance, we were probably due for a decade or two of below-trend performance (international stocks, interestingly, were below the mean, so, there, the firm's assumption might have been low). It was always possible, of course, that stock and bond performance for the next ten years would equal or exceed performance for the last ten. More likely, however, we were in the early years of a ten-year to twenty-year "regression" in which the returns on financial assets would disappoint.

So what might alternative assumptions have looked like? After consulting the work of a few gurus of mean-regression— Jeremy Grantham of Grantham, Mayo, Van Otterloo, & Co., Robert Shiller of Yale University, and Andrew Smithers of Smithers & Co., here was what I came up with. As with any financial estimates, mine were subjective and imprecise and represented no more than one guess as to how the future might unfold.

Asset Class	Firm Assumptions	My Assumptions
T-bills	4.5%	4.0%
Municipal Bonds	7.2%	4.5%
International Stocks	4.5%	6.0%
U.S. Stocks	11.8%	2.0%
Funds of Funds	9.8%	5.0%

Would these changes have an impact on the median projected return of my hypothetical portfolio? Yes.

Median annual return using the brokerage firm's assumptions: 9%.

Median annual return using my assumptions: 4%.

Well, 4% a year was a far cry from 9%, but the brokerage firm was still going to make me money, right? Yes, probably, but less than the amount suggested by either of the estimates. Once again, the wisdom lay in the fine print: *"Returns are shown before the deduction of fees . . . and assume reinvestment of income and no transaction costs or taxes"* (my italics).

2) Beware of Costs

My brokerage firm included a detailed disclosure of fees (but not taxes), which many firms don't. Despite its cost disclosure, however, the firm left it up to me to figure out what such fees would mean for my projected returns.

The fees on my proposed investment program ranged from 0.5% on cash to an astronomical 3% plus on funds of funds. In aggregate, these fees amounted to about 1.5% of assets per year—painful but typical. The firm didn't say one word about taxes, but these would eat another two to three percentage points of my return. And then, of course, there was inflation.

To convert the firm's projections into realistic projections, I assumed that, on average, each year, fees and transaction costs would consume 1.5% of my money; taxes 20% of gains, income and dividends, (a relatively low number, thanks to the tax-exempt municipal bonds); and inflation 3.0% of assets.

On the brokerage firm's assumed median return of 9%, this would result in an expected pre-inflation net return of about 6% per year and a net increase in purchasing power of about 3%—less than the advertised rate, but nothing to sniff at. On my assumed median return of 4%, however, the pre-inflation expected return would only be about 2% per year, with a net loss of purchasing power of 1% a year. For every $100,000 invested, I would probably have about $120,000 in ten years, which would be worth about $90,000 in today's dollars.

Back-of-the-Envelope Real Returns
The Impact of Costs and Inflation

Cost	Brokerage Firm Estimate	My Estimate
Gross Return	9.0%	4.0%
LESS:		
Transaction Costs	0.5%	0.5%
Fees	1.0%	1.0%
Taxes	20.0%	20.0%
Net Return	6.0%	2.0%
Inflation	3.0%	3.0%
Actual Return	3.0%	−1.0%

Lest this sound depressing, it's worth noting what would happen if I were to do nothing—if I just buried the $100,000 in the backyard. I wouldn't pay costs, fees or taxes. Thanks to inflation, however, when I dug the money up again, it would be worth only $74,000.

3) Beware of Stock Picking

Some people still persist in believing that a good stockbroker should help you pick good stocks. If you still believe this, stop. The last reason you should hire an investment advisor is to help you pick stocks.

Most investment advisors have dozens of things to worry about before they get around to picking stocks: Recruiting new clients, coaxing new money out of old clients, schmoozing, hand-holding, keeping up-to-date on a torrent of new products and deals, monitoring positions, executing trades, moving money, processing paperwork, pleasing bosses, managing assistants, attending "compliance" seminars, picking funds. If not for technology, most advisors would barely have time to follow the market, let alone analyze stocks. An advisor might be aided by the work of the firm's research analysts, but even this won't be enough to help him consistently pick stocks that beat the market. Big firms have hundreds of analysts covering thousands of securities in dozens of markets. Every client is different, so even if analysts were always right (they aren't) and even if "buy" ratings meant you should buy the stock (they don't), your advisor would have to sift through hundreds of *buys* to find the best ones.

And this isn't even the real problem. The real problem is that, in any stock picking effort, your advisor (and you) will be competing with thousands upon thousands of full-time professionals engaged in nothing but trying to find and exploit tiny information advantages that other full-time professionals miss. The professionals are smart, nimble, experienced, well trained, well equipped and deeply plugged in, so much so that they often finish exploiting valuable information before you, your advisor or CNBC even know it exists.

As described, the advantage of professional investors is not (usually) the result of lax regulation or corruption and, therefore, is not something that can be fixed by a "level playing field." It is the result of a hyper-competitive industry staffed by career professionals trying as hard as they legally can to win. Weekend cyclists rarely imagine that they could hop on a bike and win the Tour de France. Similarly, beer-league softball players rarely imagine that they could step onto a "level playing field" and play for the Yankees. For a variety of reasons, however, many casual investors imagine that, with minimal effort, they can ride wheel-to-wheel with the Lance Armstrongs and Derek Jeters of investing.

But what about *information*? Aren't good stockbrokers supposed to give you "tips"? Aren't they supposed to chat with the firm's traders and analysts and figure out what the "smart money" is doing—so you can do it first? Maybe, but the value of such information is overrated. Even if your broker's trading-floor buddies know more than you do, they don't know what stocks are going to do. Worse, if your broker does manage to unearth a tidbit of truly valuable information—a tip unknown to most investors, one that enables you to make money—he will merely be helping you commit a crime (insider trading). The SEC defines "material non-public information" as anything that the average investor might want to know when considering a trade. If you trade while in possession of such information, you're breaking the law.

As with fund managers, only a handful of advisors have the skill, information and discipline necessary to beat the market over the long haul. Unfortunately, the time it will take you to determine whether your advisor is a member of this elite group will render the effort irrelevant. The proof will not be that the advisor occasionally picks stocks that go up: Remember, stocks can only go two ways—up or down—and lots of people look good with fifty-fifty odds. The proof will be that the advisor's picks exceed the performance of an appropriate market benchmark on a risk-adjusted basis *after all costs* over decades (the time it takes to eliminate the possibility of the performance being luck). And long before then, of course, if the advisor really is a proto-Buffett, he or she will have decamped for a hedge fund.

4) Beware of Fund and Manager Picking

Warning: This is hard to swallow. Intuitively, it seems perfectly reasonable to expect that a team of experts dedicated to doing nothing other than evaluating professional money managers would be able to identify some who will consistently beat the market. Do not let the apparent reasonableness of this claim persuade you that your advisors will be able to do this, however, because there's little evidence to suggest that they will.

One problem is that most such manager assessments are based on past performance, and, as the disclaimers say, past performance does not tell you much about future returns. In any given period, some funds will beat their benchmarks. Without decades of history and detailed data about holdings, style, and other factors, however, it is hard to tell whether the performance was the result of luck or skill. Superior past performance, moreover, *does not meaningfully increase the likelihood of superior future performance.* Thus, analyses that rely on past performance as a way of selecting funds are usually flawed. Put differently, you don't want to buy funds that *have* performed well, you want to buy funds that *will* perform well. And if your advisor's logic is that the chosen funds *will* perform well because they *have* performed well, he or she is deluded.

It would be helpful to be able to cite a single study that proves this once and for all, but academics have struggled with the relevance of past performance for nearly thirty years. Early studies found *no* correlation between past performance and future returns. More recent studies have found some minor examples of correlation, but mostly on the laggard end of the scale (i.e., crappy funds tend to stay crappy). Some studies have found examples of performance persistence at both the high and low ends, but others have concluded that most of this persistence was the result of expenses, style, momentum and other market-related factors, not skill. In any event, academics have not yet determined conclusively that superior past performance predicts superior future performance, much less that an investor can use past performance to select funds or managers that will generate superior future returns.

Of course, when selecting managers, your advisors will consider many factors in addition to past performance. They will establish minimum track records and fund sizes. They will review methodologies, disciplines, financial controls and compliance records. They will analyze benchmark correlation and risk-adjusted returns. They will interview individuals, scrutinize educational backgrounds. They will evaluate portfolio turnover. They will monitor ongoing performance. They will rank all 20,000-plus U.S. managers on these and other "stringent quantitative and qualitative requirements." In short, they will do many (but not all) of the things that a reasonable person might do to try to identify managers and funds likely to deliver superior future returns. But will they succeed? Who knows?

No advisor I reviewed provided evidence showing that it could select funds or managers that had a better-than-even chance of beating the market. No advisor disclosed the performance of *all* funds in a given category versus its chosen funds, or even the *number* of chosen funds (ten, a hundred, a thousand, ten thousand?). No advisor disclosed how much of a commission it got for selling a particular manager or fund, as well as what role this commission played in the selection process. No advisor disclosed what percentage of last year's recommended funds outperformed their benchmarks *this* year, or whether the average winner outperformed by more than the average loser lagged (a critical consideration). No advisor disclosed whether last year's recommended funds were the *same* as this year's, or whether the advisor will recommend that you switch to new funds every year, thus generating obscene transaction and tax costs. No advisor evaluated managers on *expense ratios*, one factor that *has* been shown to have predictive value.

To illustrate the problem, let's say your advisor winnows the field of 20,000-plus managers to a hundred and identifies managers with a fifty-fifty chance of beating their benchmarks (significantly better than the average of all managers). In Year One, half of the recommended managers (fifty) will beat their benchmarks and half won't (fifty). If you have bought an outperformer, your advisor will pat herself on the back. If you have bought a laggard, your advisor might say that the manager had a disappointing year and is "under review." In Year Two, twenty-five of the original fifty outperformers will outperform again—obviously superior funds!—and the other twenty-five will have a disappointing year. Of the original laggards, meanwhile, twenty-five will outperform ("back on track!") and twenty-five will lag ("another disappointing year. . . "). If you have the misfortune of owning one of the twenty-five two-year laggards, your advisor might explain that the firm has purged the fund from its recommended list and suggest that you dump it and buy a better one. Meanwhile, the advisor will have found another twenty-five managers with good past performance to replace the twenty five that have gone to the dogs.

Part of the problem is that most advisors try to select winning *managers*, instead of winning *disciplines* (such as indexing). Even if they identify bona fide past winners, therefore, this is no guarantee that something critical to the winning performance won't soon change—leaving you with a fistful of frightfully ordinary funds (and facing a big transaction and tax hit if you decide to ditch them). For example:

- The portfolio manager responsible for the past returns might leave. Why? Because he might be bored. Or dynastically wealthy. Or annoyed that his bosses are gliding along on his coattails and eager to start his own firm.
- The portfolio manager might begin to relax, devoting the night- and weekend-time he once spent researching stocks to researching art auctions or private-jet cabin design.
- The fund or management firm, having posted fantastic returns, might be swamped with new capital, which will lead to diseconomies of scale (and lower future returns).
- The fund or management firm might raise fees (which will act as a drag on future returns).
- The temporary market conditions that led to several spectacular years might change, leaving a talented growth-stock manager flailing in a value-stock market, or vice versa.

The bottom line is, although common sense suggests that scrutinizing past performance and qualitative measures should enable you to select superior funds and managers, there is little evidence suggesting that it will. There is plenty of evidence, meanwhile, suggesting that paying an advisor to pick high-cost active funds will result in a higher expense burden than if you simply bought a low-cost passive fund.

And there is also plenty of evidence that a lower expense burden is indicative of superior future returns. So until advisors trot out some compelling data about the value of their active-manager selection services, there seems no reason to shell out for them.

Mutual Funds

We turn now to the other investment product familiar to most individual investors: the mutual fund. What is a mutual fund? A cheap way to hire a professional financial advisor? A safe way to own stocks? An easy way to pick winners? A simple way to make sure you are diversified?

No.

A mutual fund is a pool of money managed in a prescribed manner. That's it. Mutual funds can be a convenient way to manage all or a portion of your portfolio, akin to using prefabricated components when constructing a house. Most mutual funds are not, however, adequately diversified portfolios in and of themselves, and they aren't tailored to your particular needs. Mutual funds are also not "safe." Some mutual funds are so risky or expensive, in fact, that buying them is like volunteering to get mugged.

Similarly, a mutual fund manager is *not* a financial advisor. He does not evaluate your cash flows, goals, assets, risk tolerance and time horizon and help you construct a portfolio with an appropriate risk/return profile. He does not know who you are—or care. He doesn't know how you might best achieve your financial goals. He doesn't know how much volatility you can stand or how much you can afford to lose.

Why is this important? Because, *used intelligently*, mutual funds are powerful tools. They allow investors with little money and time to pool resources and benefit from the same information, clout, expertise, and economies of scale as big institutions. They provide some diversification (within the criteria of the fund), without the hassle and cost of acquiring and managing individual securities. They can help you construct and run your portfolio more easily, cheaply and quickly than you can on your own.

Alas, mutual funds are often *not* used intelligently. They are often seen as tools to "make money" or "beat the market." They are often chosen without regard to asset allocation. They are often selected on the basis of past performance, favorable press reviews, advertising, brand familiarity and other criteria that have little or no predictive value. They are often bought with no attention to the impact of costs and tax efficiency, which *do* have predictive value. They are often thought to be doing well when they are doing poorly (lagging a benchmark in an up market), and, conversely, thought to be doing poorly when they are doing well (beating a benchmark in a down market). They are often held for a year or two when they should be held for decades.

As described earlier, in a diversified portfolio, the most important decision is *asset allocation*: Placing an appropriate amount of your portfolio in stocks, bonds, cash, and real estate. Because appropriate allocation depends on your goals, time horizon and risk tolerance, fund managers are not—and cannot be—responsible for this process. All they can do is offer a vehicle with which to *implement* allocation decisions.

Top Ten Rules of Mutual Fund Self-Defense

- Don't confuse fund managers with financial advisors—fund managers do not know or care what is right for you
- Only use funds as carefully chosen elements of a total portfolio
- Shop on price: Cheaper is almost always better
- Think long and hard before buying an active fund over a passive fund
- Never buy a fund that charges a 12b–1 fee or load
- Only rarely—and for very good reason—buy index funds that charge more than a 0.20% expense ratio and active funds that charge more than 0.50%
- Unless you are buying an index fund, don't pay much attention to past performance—it doesn't persist
- If you are buying an index fund, pay enormous attention to past performance (relative to the benchmark)—it *does* persist
- Ignore pretax returns; focus on *after-tax* returns
- Never sell a fund without considering the tax consequences

If the stock market crashes and your fund tanks, in other words, it won't be your fund manager's fault. Similarly, if you put all your eggs in a superhot energy fund basket and energy stocks blow up, you will have only yourself to blame. The sooner you understand this, the sooner you can stop blaming your fund manager for losses that aren't her fault. And, just as important, the sooner you can *start* blaming her for losses that *are* her fault. These include under-performing passive benchmarks, charging egregious fees, racking up huge tax bills, and, in most cases, *hurting you instead of helping you*.

At last count, there were more than 8,000 mutual funds in the United States alone. Why so many? Because the mutual fund business is a great business. The investing public has an insatiable appetite for ways to play the market, so fund companies can profitably supply new funds every year. The investing public, moreover, does not have an enviable ability to discern quality funds from crap, so even wealth-destroying misfits can generate fees for decades. In the equity category alone, there are 5,000 funds, one for every U.S. stock.

Funds come in every conceivable persuasion, categorized (loosely), in many different ways:

- *Asset class*: Stocks, bonds, money markets, real estate (REITs), commodities and asset allocation (multiple asset classes).
- *Geography*: United States, international, regional, country specific and emerging markets.
- *Objective*: Growth (capital appreciation), growth and income (capital appreciation and dividends), income (dividends), tax-managed (focus on after-tax performance), life cycle (asset allocation shifts as you age), absolute return (goal of positive appreciation in any market).
- *Style*: Size (small-cap, large-cap, mid-cap, micro-cap), value (cheap stocks), growth (fast-growing companies regardless of price), sector (industry-focused), quantitative and "contrarian" (tries to bet against consensus).
- *Type*: Active (tries to pick good securities), passive (buys all securities that meet preset criteria).

- *Cost*: Sales commissions ("load") or no sales commissions ("no load"), distribution and service fees, advisory fees, redemption fees, account maintenance fees and order processing fees.

How can you even begin to choose? Mostly, you can't, at least not in a way sure to produce market-beating returns. You can, however, increase your odds.

What you want in a fund is the highest possible after-tax, risk-adjusted, *expected* return (relative to the appropriate benchmark). You should not care much about past returns. You should not care about pretax returns, unless you are buying the fund in a tax-sheltered account. You should not care much about favorable reviews, Morningstar "stars," and other third-party recommendations, because these will not consistently improve your odds.

What will? Choosing low-cost, passively managed index funds, which usually beat the majority of funds in their peer groups. Or, if you must play the active-management game, focusing on *price* and *size*. Expensive funds tend to do worse than cheap ones, and small funds tend to do better than big ones.

Expenses matter because, regardless of what form they take, they reduce your return. The evidence that size matters is less conclusive, but studies suggest that, especially among funds focused on small stocks, smaller funds have an advantage because they are more nimble and have more stocks from which to choose.

Past performance does have modest predictive power, at least over short time frames, but mostly for bad funds—they stay bad. Top performing funds do show a tendency to remain above-average, but, as discussed, this is largely the result of market, asset class, style and other temporary factors, as well as expense ratios, which are permanent. Moreover, because superior performance usually only persists for a year or so, you would have to switch funds every year to take advantage of it, incurring significant trading and tax costs. Studies suggest that this strategy would only make sense for investors with time frames of less than a decade, and success would be far from guaranteed.

With this in mind, here are two strategies for increasing your fund-picking odds:

Strategy One: Eliminate the most expensive 75% of funds. Eliminate the worst 25% of past performers. Eliminate funds sponsored by publicly owned firms. (They must generate a profit to please impatient shareholders, and this comes out of your pocket.) Favor funds sponsored by nonprofit firms like Vanguard and TIAA-CREF. (Even private firms have to make a profit.) Favor smaller funds over bigger ones (except when buying index funds). Throw darts.

Strategy Two: Buy low-cost index funds.

Money for Nothing

The mutual fund scandals a few years ago missed the industry's real problem. To wit: The majority of funds collect an aggregate of tens of billions of dollars a year in fees to accomplish nothing (or worse).

For the first half century of the fund industry's history (1920s–1970s), when the sources of investment returns were less well understood, mutual funds provided a welcome and apparently valuable service: A simple way is for amateur investors to own stocks picked by professionals. Unfortunately, since then, another thirty years of academic research has shown that, in most cases, this service is *not* valuable, at least the stock picking part. Why? Because investors can now invest in low-cost index funds that consistently beat professional stock pickers, especially after tax.

The problem is not with mutual funds, per se. Although there are now vehicles, such as Exchange-Traded Funds (ETFs), that are, in some cases, superior, the standard fund structure still has its place. The problem is with the stock picking.

The key to appreciating this is to stop seeing absolute fund performance as the product of the fund manager's efforts. In most cases, absolute performance—whether the fund goes up or down—is the product of the *benchmark's* performance, not the fund manager's performance. If the benchmark goes up, most funds that own stocks in the benchmark will go up. Similarly, if the benchmark goes down, most funds that own stocks in the benchmark will go down. The fund manager is not responsible for these moves. With most funds, the only performance that the fund manager is responsible for is *relative* performance. If the fund beats the benchmark, the fund has added value (either through luck or skill). If the fund lags the benchmark, the fund has *subtracted* value.

A low-cost passive fund—a fund designed to track a benchmark by buying all the stocks in the benchmark—allows investors to achieve the benchmark return with little risk of failure. Now that passive funds exist, the only reason to buy an active fund is to try to beat the benchmark. If an active fund fails to beat its benchmark, therefore, it has cost you money, even if it is up 30% for the year. Similarly, if the fund beats the benchmark, it has saved you money, even if it is *down* 30% for the year.

As discussed, most active funds fail. They don't view themselves as having failed—and they don't *say* they have failed—but this is because the fund companies are smart enough not to set an explicit goal of beating a passive benchmark. Instead, they set fuzzy goals like "capital appreciation" or "current income." If your general equity fund has lagged the S&P 500 by two percentage points per year over the last decade, the fund company might tell you that "your fund has gained an average of 8% per year for the past ten years." Another way of describing the same performance, however, might be: "We cost you 2% per year versus what you would have earned if you had just bought a low-cost S&P 500 fund. Our well-paid fund managers, administrators, distributors and salespeople thank you."

Many commentators wrongly blame the failure of active managers on incompetence and stupidity, which encourages laypeople to believe that they can do better if they just pick stocks themselves. The real reasons, therefore, are worth a closer look.

Most fund managers lag benchmarks because:

- In aggregate, returns on actively managed money will always lag passive benchmarks, and mutual funds constitute a large percentage of actively managed money. (Most of the rest is pension funds, hedge funds, trust companies and other institutions.)
- The market is pretty efficient, so gaining a consistent advantage is hard.
- The only way to beat benchmarks is to consistently outtrade other smart, well-trained, well-informed active managers, which is also hard.
- Funds that do beat benchmarks attract more capital, which makes it harder to beat benchmarks in the future.

- Benchmarks do not pay research, trading or portfolio management costs, and active managers do.
- Benchmarks do not make mistakes, and active managers do.
- Benchmarks are always fully invested, and active managers aren't.

Beating a benchmark, in other words, is not just a matter of picking stocks that beat the benchmark. It is a matter of picking stocks that beat the benchmark *by enough to offset the costs of picking them*. As discussed, these costs include trading commissions and advisory fees. They also include the cost of keeping a small percentage of the portfolio in cash. (In most years, stocks outperform cash, so cash reduces a fund's returns relative to a benchmark composed only of stocks.)

In *The Journal of Finance* in August 2000, professor Russ Wermers analyzed the stock holdings of mutual funds from 1975 to 1994. Wermers observed that, on a net basis, the funds lagged the market by about 1% per year. Wermers also concluded, however, that the fund managers picked stocks that outperformed the market by 1.3 percentage points per year—suggesting that, when costs are ignored, mutual fund stock picking *does* add value. Alas, costs can't be ignored, and, on average, the fund managers incurred costs of 2.3% per year, resulting in the 1% lag. Of the costs, 1.6% resulted from transaction costs and management fees and 0.7% from the poor relative performance of nonstock fund holdings (cash). So, Wermers's findings suggest that active fund managers *are* skilled enough to beat the market—they're just not skilled enough to cover the costs of doing it.

Passive investing has costs, too, of course: trading costs, salary costs, overhead costs, cash-on-hand costs, tracking-error costs. It also requires skilled managers, who are expensive. On balance, however, passive investing costs less than active investing.

Active Funds (e.g., Most Funds) Are Simply a Bad Bet

Yes, some active funds beat their benchmarks (as anyone who owns one will tell you). And, yes, when they do, friends and colleagues who own them—and advisors who recommended them—will make you feel like an idiot for buying a passive fund. As long as you chose an efficient, well-run passive fund, however, you made the smart choice. The odds were in your favor.

To put some meat on this, let's look in more detail at a study I mentioned earlier, one conducted by First Quadrant L.P., a research and advisory firm. First Quadrant analyzed the performance of all general equity funds in the ten-, fifteen- and twenty-year periods through 1998, on both a pretax and after-tax basis. They then compared this performance to that of the Vanguard S&P 500 Fund. For diehard stock pickers, the results weren't pretty:

Percentage of Funds That Beat/Lagged the Vanguard S&P 500 Fund Through 1998 (Pretax Returns)

	Beat Vanguard	Margin	Lagged Vanguard	Margin
10 Years:	14%	+1.90%	86%	−3.87%
15 Years:	5%	+1.10%	95%	−3.76%
20 Years:	22%	+1.35%	78%	−2.64%

Note that the odds did not favor choosing an active fund in *any* period. Even in the best period, twenty years, you had only a 1-in-5 shot of picking a fund that beat the Vanguard S&P 500 fund. In the worst period, fifteen years, your odds dropped to 1-in-20.

Just as important, the "payoff" for the long-shot active-fund bet never came close to compensating for its risk. Over the twenty-year period, the average "winner" beat the Vanguard fund by 1.35% per year, far from enough to justify the 1-in-5 odds of selecting it. The average loser, meanwhile, which you had a 4-in-5 chance of selecting, lagged the index by –2.64% per year.

In every one of these periods, and in every period covered by almost every study I have seen, the "expected outcome" of choosing an active fund over a low-cost passive fund has been negative. In all likelihood, this will not change: In aggregate, actively managed money will always under-perform passive benchmarks, and mutual funds manage an ever-greater percentage of actively managed money. Again, this does not mean that you won't get lucky and pick a winning fund. It just means that, if you choose an active strategy over a passive one, you are betting against the odds.

In recent years, as the superiority of passive investing has become clear, the passion of those who have seen the light often resembles religious zealotry: "Markets can't be beat." "Warren Buffett and Peter Lynch were just lucky." "Everyone who works on Wall Street is a con artist or charlatan." Such statements undermine the credibility of the passive-investing movement, but the evidence suggests that, on balance, the passive approach is the wise one.

Ultimately, choosing a passive fund over an active fund is less important than choosing a low-cost fund (of either variety) over a high-cost one. If, for you, the probability of losing at least 1% of return per year by choosing an active fund is offset by the (small) possibility of picking a "winner," then go active. But do it knowing that your odds stink.

How Do We Charge Thee? Let Us Count the Ways

According the Investment Company Institute, the average equity fund fee in 2005 was 1.54% of assets—enough to chop your fifty-year return in half. ICI pointed out that the *asset-weighted* average fee was "only" 0.91%, meaning that more money was invested at the cheaper end of the scale. Of course, with a total of $4.9 *trillion* invested in equity mutual funds, even the asset-weighted figure means that investors are paying $45 billion in equity fund fees each year, most of which is wasted.

To put this in perspective, merely cutting the average fee in half would save equity fund investors $23 billion a year. If only one year's savings were dumped into a low-cost index fund, it would compound to $1 trillion in forty years. If *each* year's savings were invested in the fund, it would reach $11 trillion in forty years. This is more than twice as much as all the money currently invested in equity mutual funds. It is also more than enough to offset the entire Social Security deficit.

How can you figure out what your mutual funds cost? You can't, unfortunately, glance at a simple, dollar-based price tag—one reason so few investors know or care about price. If fund companies had to send out bill every month, the way many businesses do, fund customers would probably be more exercised about fees. Instead, fund companies just quietly scoop off a percentage of your account each quarter and show you the net return. This is so painless that some fund customers probably don't even know they are paying fees, much less what the fees are. But the impact is enormous.

You can calculate a dollar-based price tag for a mutual fund, but you have to do some work. Specifically, you have to go digging around in the fund's prospectus, find the section on costs and fees, make adjustments to adapt the amounts to your situation, and then factor in what you will lose because the fees will no longer compound in your account—an indirect cost you won't find in the prospectus.

Whatever you do, don't ignore a complex fee structure just because you can't be bothered to decipher it. There is *no reason* to buy an expensive fund. If your broker's persuasions have you leaning in that direction, however, ask him or her to give you a spreadsheet showing exactly how much the fund will cost you (in dollars *and* lost compounding) over the anticipated life of your investment. If he or she is too lazy to do this, figure it out on your own. As one of my former colleagues is fond of saying, many people spend a year researching a $25,000 car purchase and a minute researching a $25,000 investment. Don't be one of them.

To figure out how much a mutual fund really costs, get the prospectus and find the section called "Fees and Expenses." In this section, you will find a chart with several categories of fees. You may also find a chart with several categories of *share classes*, with different fees for each class. If you buy the fund, you will be buying a single share class, so it behooves you to analyze the costs of each of them. (Ostensibly, share classes are designed to give you, the customer, more options. In reality, they will just make you want to throw the prospectus out the window.)

The "Fees and Expenses" charts might include some or all of the following costs:

- *Front-End Load*: Also known as a sales commission. A front-end load is a percentage of your investment that is taken right off the top, that will never be invested in anything. This charge can range from 0% to a staggering 8%, and it is used to compensate brokers, their firms and, sometimes, other intermediaries for persuading you to choose that fund instead of 9,000 others. View a front-end load the way you would a skull-and-crossbones on a vat of chemicals. *Never buy a fund that charges one.*

- *Back-End Load*: Also known as a "Contingent Deferred Sales Charge" (CDSC). This is another sales commission, assessed when you sell the fund instead of (or in addition to) when you buy it. Sometimes this charge declines each year you own the fund and then disappears. Treat a back-end load the same way you treat a front-end load. *Never buy a fund that charges one, unless you are sure you will keep the fund until the end of the contingency period.*

- *12b–1 Fee*: Also known as a "distribution and servicing fee." Another sales commission mechanism, designed to compensate your financial advisor, his or her firm, and other intermediaries on an ongoing basis, and to also pay for your fund firm's advertising. The 12b–1 fee was invented when fund shoppers intelligently learned to avoid funds with loads. 12b–1 fees are assessed each year, as a percentage of assets, so many fund customers don't know they're there. Depending on how long you hold the fund, a 12b–1 fee can be even more damaging than a load, and, collectively, fund investors paid $11 billion of them in 2005. *Never buy a fund that charges one.*

- *Advisory or Management Fee*: A percentage-of-assets fee used primarily to pay the fund's portfolio manager, traders and research team. You can't avoid paying an advisory fee, and you shouldn't object to the concept of paying one. (This is what you are hiring the fund to do, after all: Manage your money.) You should, however, make sure this fee is as low as possible. Preferably below 0.50% of assets per year, lower if you're buying an index fund.

- *Other Expense Fee*: This category allows the fund company to sock you with everything they haven't been able to stuff into another fee category (including, if necessary, their profit margin). They don't have to tell you what the "other" expenses are, and you probably don't want to know.

- *Expense Ratio*: The 12b–1 fee, advisory fee and other expense fees together constitute the fund's "Expense Ratio." If you don't want to bother looking at all the separate expense categories, you can learn most of what you need to know from this ratio.

- *Redemption Fee*: Assessed if the fund is sold within a certain period, and, therefore, similar to a back-end load. Designed to discourage market timers and other short-term traders and, therefore, reasonable. Still, do not buy a fund with a redemption fee unless you are confident you won't have to pay it.

- *Order Processing Fee*: Adding insult to injury, some fund companies charge a small transaction fee for the privilege of buying or selling the fund.

Those are some common fund fees and costs. There are others, too, of course. Chief among them? Lost compounding of fees and, in taxable accounts, taxes (see below). Advocates of expensive funds will often argue that you get what you pay for, that expensive funds are better. This is usually a crock. On average, the less you pay, the better your returns.

Don't Forget Taxes

Unless you plan to hold your mutual funds in a tax-sheltered account, you should focus on *after-tax returns*. Most funds tout only pretax returns, however, so focusing on after-tax performance requires you to go digging around in the prospectus again.

The First Quadrant study I mentioned earlier analyzed both pretax and after-tax returns. As bad as the pretax numbers were—in the twenty years through 1998, only one in five U.S. equity funds beat Vanguard's S&P 500 fund—the after-tax performance was worse. Why? Because actively managed funds trade more often than index funds, and trading usually increases tax costs. First Quadrant concluded that, after tax, only 16% of funds did better than the index.

First Quadrant's study also analyzed the average under-performance that was directly attributable to poor tax management: 0.56% of return per year. Doesn't sound like much? On a $100,000 investment, at a 10% rate of return, even a

–0.56% annual lag would end up costing you $130,000 over twenty-five years.

Tax costs come in several flavors: short-term capital gains (positions sold in less than one year), long-term capital gains (positions sold after more than one year), dividends and deferred capital gains (eventual sale of fund shares). Under the current tax code, by far the most expensive is short-term capital gains. Once federal, state and local tax collectors have taken their cuts, investors in the top tax bracket can end up keeping less than half of their short-term returns.

The first rule of tax management, therefore, is to avoid taking short-term gains. This means either never selling winning stocks or funds held for less than a year, or always offsetting such gains with short-term losses. The failure to follow this simple rule clobbers the after-tax performance of many mutual funds. As I'll discuss in the next chapter, the same practice often dooms today's hottest investment vehicle—the hedge fund—to after-tax mediocrity.

A fund's annual turnover can give you an idea of how tax-efficient it is likely to be (generally, the more turnover, the more taxes). The best way to assess tax-efficiency, however, is to check the after-tax performance figures—which, thankfully, funds are now required to report.

A Fund-Picking Exercise

For some self-defense practice, let's look at a couple of examples. The two funds below were not picked at random—I chose the fund families based on the preconception that one would be expensive and the other cheap, and then I clicked through to two similar-sounding funds. These funds were the first and only two I looked at, however (i.e., I didn't go hunting for an astronomically expensive outlier). To focus on price rather than style, I chose two "active" funds: Each has a research team and stock picking portfolio manager. Each also bears the name "Morgan," in case the invocation of the archetypal Wall Street power broker makes you feel more comfortable.

Fund One: Morgan Stanley Growth Fund

Sponsor: Morgan Stanley, a for-profit, publicly-owned investment banking, brokerage and asset management firm

Objective: Seeks long-term growth of capital (and a profit for Morgan Stanley)

Strategy: Invests primarily in "growth-oriented" stocks, mostly with market capitalizations of $1 billion or more. Focuses on companies with consistent or rising earnings growth, strong free cash flow and compelling business strategies

Type: Active (team of stock pickers tries to pick winners)

Share Classes: A, B, C and D

Size (All Classes): Approximately $700 million

Annual Turnover: 125% (Average 2002–2006)

Expense Ratio: 1.82%–0.82% of assets per year, depending on share class, plus loads and other fees

Pretax Returns (10 Years through 2005): 7.17% per year

After-Tax Returns (10 Years through 2005): 5.50% per year

Pretax Return Relative to a Growth Index Fund:* –1.35% per year

---

*Compares the performance of the fund with that of the Vanguard Growth Index Fund (a low-cost passive fund) over the same period. The "After-Tax" return for both funds is after taxes on dividends and capital gains and the sale of fund shares.

After-Tax Return Relative to Growth Index Fund: −1.81% per year

Fees and Costs

Class A Shares: Front-end load (sales commission) of up to 5.25% of invested capital and a 0.25% 12b−1 fee.** Expense ratio of 1.07% (on top of the initial sales charge), composed of an advisory fee of 0.50% per year and an other expense fee of 0.32%. Also, an order processing fee of $5.25.

Class B Shares: No front-end load, but a back-end load of up to 5.00% if you sell within the first five years (declining by 1.00% per year before disappearing in year six). Expense ratio of a stinging 1.82%, composed of a 12b−1 fee of 1.00%, an advisory fee of 0.50%, and an other expense fee of 0.32%. (Plus the order processing fee.) After eight years, Class B Shares convert to Class A shares, resulting in a reduced 12b−1 fee and, therefore, a lower expense ratio of 1.07%.

Class C Shares: No front-end load and a smaller back-end load than the Class B Shares—1.00% if sold within eighteen months. However, an outrageous expense ratio of 1.79%, composed of a 12b−1 fee of 0.97% and the normal advisory and other expense fees of 0.50% and 0.32% (plus the order processing fee). Class C shares look comparatively cheap—until you realize that Class C shares never convert to Class A shares and therefore maintain their 1.79% expense ratio forever.

Class D Shares: No sales charges and—imagine this—no 12b−1 fee. After the standard 0.50% Advisory fee and 0.32% Other fee, you get an ongoing expense ratio of an almost-reasonable 0.82%. This is still high, relative to a low-cost fund, but it is the only sane choice in

(continued)

**The front-end load declines as the size of the investment increases: 4.75% for $25,000-plus, 4% for $50,000-plus, 3% for $100,000-plus, 2% for $500,000-plus, etc. There is no load on investments larger than $1 million.

the bunch. Alas, you need a minimum of $5,000,000 to buy the Class D shares.

All Share Classes: High tax costs. With 125% annual turnover, the fund holds its average position for only ten months. This translates into significant short-term gains taxes. Over the past decade, the fund's tax inefficiency has knocked nearly 0.50% per year off its return relative to the growth index fund, which had 29% turnover.

Summary

The Morgan Stanley Growth Fund tries to beat the market—they don't say this, but it is implied. The fund's stock pickers are not looking for "bargains," per se, but for rapidly growing companies whose prospects they believe are underestimated. They are looking for good businesses, not lousy ones. They trade frequently, holding each stock for an average of only ten months (which begs the question: Why bother with good businesses?). They do not trade anywhere near well enough to offset their costs, in part because their costs are astronomical. The fund has lagged the growth index fund by almost 2% per year (after-tax) over the past decade.

Fund Two: Vanguard Morgan Growth Fund

Sponsor: The Vanguard Group, a "mutual company" owned by its funds and fund holders

Objective: Seeks long-term capital appreciation

Strategy: Invests mainly in mid- and large-capitalization U.S. companies whose revenues and/or earnings are expected to grow faster than average

Type: Active

Share Classes: *Investor* and *Admiral* (for accounts with $100,000 or more).

Size: $4.5 billion

Annual Turnover: 93% (average 2001–2005)

Expense Ratio: 0.41% to 0.24% of assets per year, depending on share class. No loads or other expenses.

Pretax Returns (10 Years through 2005): 9.44% per year

After-Tax Returns (10 Years through 2005): 7.35% per year

Pretax Return Relative to Growth Index Fund: +0.92% per year

After-tax Return Relative to Growth Index Fund: +0.04% per year

Fees and Costs

Investor Shares: No sales charges or 12b–1 fees. Expense ratio of 0.41%, composed of an advisory fee of 0.39% and an other expense fee of 0.02%. No order processing fee.

Admiral Shares: No sales charges or 12b–1 fees. Expense ratio of a modest 0.24%, composed of an advisory fee of 0.22%, and an other expense fee of 0.02%. No order processing fee.

All Shares: High tax costs. The fund's 93% annual turnover means that it holds its average position for slightly longer than a year, but this still generates significant short-term gains and realized long-term gains. Taxes have knocked 2% off the fund's annual return relative to that of an S&P 500 fund.

Summary

Like the Morgan Stanley Growth Fund, the Vanguard Morgan Growth Fund tries to pick winners. The fund concentrates on medium-sized and big companies with rapidly growing earnings. The fund trades frequently, but not as often as the Morgan Stanley fund. The fund charges a low fee and no sales commissions. The fund's stock pickers appear to be pretty good: They beat the growth index fund by almost

(continued)

1% per year on a pretax basis over the past ten years, and they matched it after-tax. They also beat the Morgan Stanley Growth Fund by 2.27% per year pretax, and 1.85% after-tax.

The verdict? Both funds have the same strategy: Make money by buying the stocks of fast-growing companies. Both funds try to pick stocks that will beat the market. Vanguard's stock pickers appear to be more talented than Morgan Stanley's, and more patient. The Morgan Stanley fund trades nearly twice as much as the Vanguard fund, and thus racks up higher trading and tax costs. It is also vastly more expensive.

What might the fee difference between the two funds cost you over time? Revisiting our hypothetical $100,000 account and 10% return, the decision to buy the Morgan Stanley fund's Class A shares would cost you $3,000 more *the moment you bought it* (based on a front-end load of 3%, which applies to investments between $100,000 and $250,000). This alone puts you in a hole versus Vanguard from which you will likely never recover. Assuming the same gross return for both funds, the Morgan Stanley fund will cost $6,400 more than the Vanguard fund in the first year. After five years, the relative cost difference will swell to $11,000, and, after a decade, $27,000. After fifty years, the decision to go with Morgan Stanley could be a $3.8 million mistake.

Would you do better with the "B" or "C" shares? Nope. In fact, except for the first few years, you would do worse. After five years in the B shares, you would be down $12,000 relative to Vanguard. By year eight, however, you would fall behind the A shares, and then you would track their mediocre relative performance the rest of the way. If you made the mistake of holding the C shares in perpetuity, you would get massacred (because unlike the B shares, the C shares don't convert to the cheaper A shares). Even if you were rich enough to own the D shares you would take it on the chin. A half-century of compounding at a 0.82% expense ratio (Morgan Stanley D shares) versus a 0.24% ratio (Vanguard Admiral) would put you $2.5 million behind Vanguard.

So, then, what are you getting for your extra money at Morgan Stanley? Nothing. In fact, you are almost certainly just throwing your money away. The Morgan Stanley fund has lagged the Vanguard fund in the past, and, unless Morgan Stanley drastically reduces the fund's expenses probably will in the future. What's more, if your Morgan Stanley financial advisor advised you to buy the Morgan Stanley fund, you're getting bad advice. Given the vastly higher expenses, no objective advisor would choose the Morgan Stanley fund over the Vanguard fund unless he or she was incompetent (or conflicted).

Is Morgan Stanley a Den of Thieves?

Does all this mean that Morgan Stanley is screwing you? No. The fees are all there, for anyone who cares to look them up. It does mean, however, that the firm is charging an outrageous price for an inferior product.

Morgan Stanley's pricing reflects the fact that Morgan Stanley is a for-profit corporation focused on a price-insensitive segment of the market (rich people). Morgan Stanley is run by well-paid employees who want to continue to be well-paid and owned by demanding shareholders who want to continue to earn an excellent rate of return. Morgan Stanley, therefore, needs to make a fatter profit than Vanguard or its shareholders will revolt and its employess will be fired. And Morgan Stanley is better at making a profit than it is at managing growth funds, at least in this case.

There is nothing sleazy about making a profit, and Morgan Stanley is not the first firm to target consumers for whom a premium brand and the perception of quality are more persuasive than price. Such consumers are not "rational" in the purely economic sense: They are often motivated by human factors like status, relationships, marketing, brand attributes, perceived quality, comfort, convenience and peer groups. They will pay a premium to drive BMWs, and a premium to work with Morgan Stanley financial advisors, some of whom hail from familiar educational and socio-economic backgrounds.

Of course, not everyone can afford BMWs. And, more importantly, not even people who *can* afford BMWs would drive them if they realized they were not, in fact, high-quality automobiles but just dime-a-dozen jalopies *priced* like BMWs. And that's how, in mutual funds, Morgan Stanley's high-price-for-high-quality positioning breaks down.*

The Morgan Stanley Growth Fund is Not *a BMW*

In the car world, high quality means superb handling, leather seats, side-impact airbags, reliability, service, voice-activated GPS systems, low road noise and 24–7 roadside assistance. These features cost money, so quality varies directly with price: To get a better product, you have to pay more.

In the mutual fund world, meanwhile, "high quality" means the "highest expected risk-adjusted return." Because fees directly reduce returns, quality still varies with price—but, this time, *inversely*. It is impossible to predict whether a given group of stock pickers will beat the market on a gross basis, or determine which of two groups will outperform the other. As a

---

*Morgan Stanley has a hell of a mergers and acquisitions advisory team, but if you buy the Growth Fund you're not hiring them to advise you on mergers and acquisitions.

result, the only way to assess the expected return of a fund is to look at the expense ratio. The way to get more in a mutual fund is to pay *less*. As counter-intuitive as it sounds, therefore, in a mutual fund, *high price* usually means *low quality*.

This does not mean that you should entrust your retirement to Funds4Less.com, or that, by doing business with Morgan Stanley, you won't have plenty of rich and sophisticated company. It just means that between Fund One and Fund Two—the Morgan Stanley Growth Fund and the Vanguard Morgan Growth Fund—the Vanguard fund is superior.

All of which is to say: Your Morgan Stanley financial advisor may be loyal and charming. He may be so trustworthy that his *advice* is worth paying a premium for (although I wouldn't assume this, if he's advising you to buy the Morgan Stanley Growth Fund). He may have access to *other* Morgan Stanley products and services that are worth paying up for. But if he sticks you in the Morgan Stanley Growth Fund, he's charging you a BMW price for a Yugo.

All Index Funds Are Not Created Equal

So, you're finally convinced: Passive funds are the way to go. Can you just go out and buy any old index fund?

Unfortunately, no. Index funds vary in quality as much as active funds. The best ones track their benchmarks so closely that they lose only a few basis points (hundredths of a percentage point) per year, and a few even come out ahead. The worst ones, however, are more of a rip-off than the most expensive active funds. Far from tracking their benchmarks, these lemons lose a couple of *percentage points* per year.

The good news is that many of the challenges associated with analyzing active funds disappear when analyzing index funds. You know what the appropriate benchmark is, and you know what the fund's goal is (to track it). You also know whether the fund has succeeded or failed, and by how much. With index funds, moreover, at least with S&P 500 index funds, past performance *is* indicative of future results—the funds that have most closely tracked the index in the past should most closely track it in the future.

Shop on Price: Cost Matters

As with active funds, the most important difference between index funds—and the most reliable predictor of future performance—is cost. A study of S&P 500 index funds by Edwin Elton, Martin Gruber and Jeffrey Busse found that expense ratios ranged from 0.06% to 1.35%, with a median of 0.44%, and that the cheapest fund outperformed the most expensive by more than 1.5% per year. Manager skill also matters (how the portfolio manager deals with cash inflows and outflows, transaction costs, changes in the index and incremental income from lending shares), but such skill accounts for only 0.2% of performance per year. Lastly, the funds also vary by tax efficiency, with some far more efficient than others.

Unfortunately, even investors enlightened enough to buy index funds don't appear to understand the impact of costs on performance. Specifically, they appear to be influenced by their financial advisors, who often steer them wrong. The study cited above found that, instead of buying the cheapest funds with the best past performance, index-fund investors tended to buy funds with 12b–1 fees, loads and high expense ratios—all of which reliably predict poorer performance. In other words, the fund firms' incentive marketing deals with the financial advisors appear to work.

Another study confirmed that investors don't understand the importance of fees, even when they aren't getting bad advice. James Choi (Yale), David Laibson (Harvard) and Brigitte Madrian (Wharton) asked students at Harvard Business School, Wharton and Harvard College to allocate a hypothetical portfolio among four S&P 500 index funds. The professors found that more than 95% of the students failed to minimize fees. Even when the fees were highlighted, more than 80% of the students failed to minimize them. Instead, they focused on irrelevant "absolute performance since inception" data and allocated capital to the funds that showed the highest absolute return.* The professors' conclusions:

- Investors don't understand the importance of fees to performance.
- Even when investors do understand the importance of fees, they can't find them in the prospectus.
- Highlighting fees reduces bad decisions but doesn't eliminate them.
- Investors are swayed by irrelevant but salient return information.

Indexing: More Than Just S&P 500 Funds

One reason passive investing often gets dissed is that commentators equate all such strategies with owning an S&P 500 fund. This strategy still results in the holder outperforming the

---

*In an index fund, "absolute return since inception" data is irrelevant because the funds track the index and the absolute performance is determined almost entirely by the inception date. The performance of the fund *relative* to the index is important, but the students didn't focus on that.

majority of other equity investors, a fact that indexing critics apparently don't understand. However, as described earlier, markets can be segmented into any number of indices, and index funds can be designed to track any of them.

Over the last century, small-cap stocks and value stocks have outperformed the S&P 500 by about 1% to 2% per year,* and an investor can now buy both groups through index funds. Similarly, high dividend-yielding stocks have, on a total return basis, outperformed stocks with low or no dividends, and index funds now exist that track them. Whether such "anomalies" will persist is open to debate, but index funds now allow investors to pursue a wide variety of passive strategies.

Even investment strategies that are not commonly considered "passive" have more in common with indexing than with traditional active management. For example, a recent bestseller by Joel Greenblatt called *The Little Book That Beats the Market* describes a strategy that identifies stocks with the combination of the highest return on capital and the lowest price. The screen allows investors to construct portfolios consisting of diversified groups of stocks with these characteristics, akin to an "index." While investors can't buy an index fund based on the book's strategy, they can easily build one themselves. And if the forces that allowed stocks with Greenblatt's charac-

---

*As described in Chapter 9, according to Ibbotson Associates, small stocks have outperformed large stocks by approximately 2% per year, and value stocks have outperformed growth stocks by about the same margin. Value stocks have outperformed the S&P 500, which contains both value and growth stocks, by about 1% per year.

teristics to outperform the broader market persist, this quasi-passive strategy should provide an S&P 500-beating return.*

Fundamental-Weighting:
The New Index Revolution

In recent years, a new indexing methodology has gained supporters, one that may improve on most used to date. The method, called "fundamental weighting," has been used for more than a decade by Dimensional Fund Advisors, which offers passive funds based on criteria such as price-to-book value. More recently, the merits and drawbacks of the strategy have burst into the headlines with debates between, among others, professor Jeremy Siegel of Wharton (pro) and Vanguard founder John Bogle (con).

Traditional index funds are "capitalization-weighted," meaning that the size of each stock in the index mirrors the relative size of the stock's total market capitalization. In a cap-weighted S&P 500 index, the biggest stocks—Microsoft, GE and ExxonMobil, for example—account for a major chunk of the index. Price changes in these stocks, therefore, have a

---

*Greenblatt's technique has one very comforting attribute, which is that it makes sense. Greenblatt is simply arguing that, at any given moment, some good businesses (high return on capital) will be trading at relatively low prices (low P-Es), and that, over the long haul, investors can do better by buying a basket of good businesses at low prices than by buying a basket of good *and* bad businesses at low *and* high prices, as they would in a S&P 500 or total market fund. Where Greenblatt's strategy differs from traditional active management is that there is no market-timing or fundamental-forecasting component. The strategy simply screens stocks based on historical performance data and current price.

much larger impact on the price change of the index than price changes in smaller stocks.

Another method of index construction is called "equal-weighting," in which all securities are held in equal-sized positions and, therefore, constitute the same percentage of the portfolio. Each stock in an equal-weighted S&P 500 fund amounts to one five-hundredth of the portfolio. In equal-weighted indices, the price change of any stock has the same impact as that of any other stock. When small stocks are doing better than the large ones, therefore, an equal-weighted index would outperform a capitalization-weighted index (and vice versa). One drawback of equal-weighted indices is that the portfolio must be re-balanced continuously, which generates higher costs. Another draw-back is that there often aren't enough shares of smaller stocks available to allow the fund to buy them without significantly affecting the stock's price. (It's easier to buy a million shares of GE than, say, Becton Dickinson.)

In a *fundamental*-weighted index, meanwhile, stocks are weighted not by the size of their market capitalizations or their pro rata share, but by the size of the underlying company (as measured by revenues, earnings, employees and other metrics). The theory is that, although stock mis-pricings are hard to determine on a stock by stock basis, stocks are often mis-priced, and so investors who buy a capitalization-weighted index get more of overpriced stocks and less of un-derpriced ones. Then, if the mispricings correct themselves, the index owner loses out: The overpriced stocks, which the index owner owns more of, drop, and the underpriced stocks, which the index owner owns less of, rise. An equal-weighted index doesn't have this problem, but the high transaction costs and scaling issue can offset the benefits.

Fundamental weighting makes sense from both an intuitive and empirical perspective. Dimensional's value-weighted funds have done extraordinarily well over the past ten years. Rob Arnott, a vocal advocate of applying the fundamental-weighting strategy to existing indices, concluded that a fundamental-weighted S&P 500 index would have outperformed a typical capitalization-weighted S&P 500 index by two points a year for the last fifty years, an enormous advantage. This shot across the bow of traditional indexing inspired a predictably skeptical response, and the battle is still raging. John Bogle argues that the higher transaction and tax costs necessary to maintain fundamental weights neutralize the advantage, and others have raised different objections. Still, dozens of ETFs and index funds are already based on fundamental weighting, and more are on the way.

So you see, even if you forgo active investing, you'll still be able to pick a fight. Arguments such as these, by the way, are the real investing controversies of today. Arguments about active vs. passive, mutual fund performance and other topics occasionally pawned off as "news" in the financial press have largely been settled. The odds that traditional stock picking and market-timing methods will work are so low that it is a mistake for most investors to pursue them. When confronted with evidence to this extent, however, those who make their livings actively managing money—the active mutual fund industry, for example—usually respond with silence or a dismissive snort that "academics don't get it." If there is evidence to support the latter view, it would be nice to see it. Given how successful the industry's nonresponse has been so far, however, one doubts it will be forthcoming.

Hedge Funds and Funds of Funds

When the stock market crashed, it did not go unnoticed that one group of investors did just fine: those who had bet it would crash—or, at least, had not bet that it would keep going up. After years of devastating market declines, in fact, it seemed that the only smart investment strategy was to be "market neutral"—to own good stocks and to short (bet against) bad ones. That way, you would make money regardless of what the market did. As rumors of spectacular bear market hedge fund results made the rounds, moreover, the excitement about this "new" strategy only grew. Hedge funds offered better returns and lower risk! They made you money even when the market dropped! Soon came the near-universal belief that everyone should own hedge funds.

When we ducks quack, the saying goes, Wall Street feeds us, and in the last few years, the number and variety of hedge funds has exploded. From a few hundred funds managing some $40 billion in 1990, there are now perhaps 10,000 funds managing more than $1 trillion. The funds pursue many different strategies: Equity market neutral. Long/short sector equity. Convertible arbitrage. Emerging markets. Merger arbitrage.

Distressed securities. Global macro.* Because hedge funds usually come with high risk and steep minimum investment sizes, moreover (circa $1 million per fund), vehicles designed to make it easier and safer to invest in them—aka funds of funds—have also exploded in popularity. So now, even average investors are advised to take the hedge-fund plunge. But should you?

Not unless you are really rich, really connected and really know what you are doing.

The logic includes concepts that should by now be familiar—high costs and the difficulty of choosing a top fund in advance—as well as factors that are unique to hedge funds: Higher risk, lower returns and less diversification benefit than you probably think. The best hedge funds and funds of funds, moreover, come with an additional roadblock: You can't invest in them. Many of the top funds are closed to new investors, and the ones that are open prefer to deal with massive institutions that can invest $10–$100 million apiece.

---

*"Market neutral" funds balance their portfolios between long and short stock bets to (ideally) remove the impact of market performance on the portfolio's return. Such funds often employ leverage, which increases both profits and losses. "Long/short sector" funds concentrate on specific industry sectors, such as technology or healthcare, but they also usually make market-direction bets by owning more longs than shorts, or vice versa. "Emerging markets" funds trade stocks and bonds in markets like Indonesia, Brazil and China. "Merger arbitrage" funds take advantage of the discount between the stock of a company that is about to be acquired and the announced acquisition price, betting that the merger will or won't go through. "Distressed securities" funds buy and sell the securities of companies in crisis, which often trade at a panic discount (and which often deserve that discount).

And then there's the overarching problem. To the extent there *was* a truly compelling opportunity in hedge funds, the secret is out, and thousands upon thousands of exuberant prospectors are already storming the Yukon in search of hedge-fund gold.

Back in ancient times (the mid–1990s), when there were relatively few hedge funds, the total amount of capital dedicated to each strategy was relatively small. For example, only a handful of funds specialized in going long and short technology stocks, and, because of this, there was a lot of low-hanging fruit, especially on the short side. Also, in the mid–1990s, rules about selective information dissemination were less stringent than they are today, so some funds routinely traded with what might today be described as "material" and "nonpublic" information. As a result, the top long/short tech funds made a killing.

The surest way to get rich in the investment business is to post a few years of extraordinary returns, because once investors see them, they will pitch camp outside your office and beg you to take their money. Unfortunately, the prosperity will be a mixed blessing, because, thanks to diseconomies of scale, the more cash you receive, the harder it is to repeat the performance that attracted it. (It is more difficult to earn a 25% return when you are managing $10 billion than when you are managing $10 million, if only because you need to find $2.5 billion worth of opportunities instead of $2.5 million worth.)

As the 1990s progressed, and long/short tech funds posted strong returns, the amount of capital allocated to the strategy multiplied. By the end of the decade, there were hundreds of long/short tech funds, each managing tens or hundreds of millions of dollars (or more), each expertly serviced by dozens of Wall Street firms, each staffed by platoons of brilliant analysts jetting around the globe seeking the smallest information edge. As the number of funds increased, they began to compete with each other, in addition to with mutual funds, pension funds and other traditional institutional investors. It became harder to maintain an advantage, and, thus, harder to post exciting returns—especially with technology stocks in the doldrums. In the last few years, the returns in the long/short tech strategy have dropped, disappointed investors have withdrawn money in disgust, and many funds have closed their doors.*

Sooner or later, this pattern should repeat itself with all hedge-fund strategies: Capital will gush toward strategies with attractive returns until the returns are no longer attractive. At that point, only the best funds will earn returns that justify their risks, and, as ever, these funds will be hard to identify in advance. Judging from some recent academic work, in fact, it seems that this has already begun to happen.

Professors William Fung, David A. Hsieh, Narayan Y. Naik and Tarun Ramadorai examined the returns of funds of funds (funds that own baskets of hedge funds) from 1994–2004. According to their study, the excess risk-adjusted returns (*alpha*) generated by funds of funds dropped significantly from the mid–1990s to the early 2000s.** Over the entire decade, the professors concluded, only about 1-in-5 funds of funds were able to generate *alpha* (a poor success rate, one similar

---

*Which probably means it's a good time to invest.

**The professors look at funds of funds data instead of hedge fund data because they believe it more accurately reflects the returns posted by hedge fund investors.

Top Ten Rules of Hedge Fund Self-Defense

- Don't invest in hedge funds unless you are really rich, really connected and really know what you're doing
- Don't buy "index" products designed to track hedge fund indices: They are outrageously expensive and lag the indices
- Don't forget that most hedge funds rack up huge tax bills: Focus on after-tax returns
- Don't forget that hedge funds usually trade the same markets as everyone else and that there is only so much "alpha" to go around
- Don't forget that hedge funds are riskier than you think
- Don't forget that hedge funds generate lower returns than you think
- Don't forget that hedge funds have less diversification benefit than you think
- Don't forget that many top hedge funds are closed to new investors and that these investors usually get the first crack at any spin-off funds
- Don't forget that everyone and his brother is now investing in (and starting) hedge funds
- Don't forget that funds of funds have many of the same problems as hedge funds and also charge another layer of fees

to the results of mutual funds). By 2004, moreover, the *amount* of alpha generated by the winners had significantly declined, suggesting that there was less opportunity to go around. The professors also concluded that the funds of funds with the best past performance had received the most new capital and that this new capital had had a negative impact on the funds' returns.

Lower Returns Than You Think

Everyone has heard stories about hedge funds making a killing, and some of the stories are even true: Some funds always hit the ball out of the park, regardless of what the market is doing. But what about the average hedge fund? What about even the above-average hedge fund? How do they do? Not as well as you might think.

One problem with evaluating hedge funds is that the industry hasn't been around long enough for researchers to have much confidence in the significance of its historical results. Researchers did not start gathering formal data on hedge funds until the mid–1990s, so today's analysts can study only about a decade's worth of returns (in comparison, data on mutual funds goes back at least to the 1960s). Furthermore, unlike the mutual fund industry, which has strict reporting standards, hedge funds aren't required to publish results. The major databases of hedge fund performance, therefore, suffer from severe reporting biases, which most researchers conclude have significantly overstated the industry's results.*

For example, according to professors Fung and Hsieh, one of the major hedge fund performance databases (TASS) reports that from 1994–2004, the average annual hedge fund return was an impressive 14.4%, net of fees. After adjusting for

---

*These biases include "survivorship bias" and "incubation bias." Survivorship bias, which also affects mutual fund data, occurs when dead or closed funds are dropped from the database and are no longer included in long-term performance averages. Many funds die because their performance was awful, so once such funds are stripped from the data, the average performance looks better than it really was. Incubation bias, meanwhile, results from the practice of hedge fund companies starting multiple funds internally and only reporting results for the ones that do well (while closing the ones that do badly).

two major biases, however, Fung and Hsieh concluded that the average performance was only 10.5%, close to the return for the S&P 500. The average performance for the fund of funds industry over the period, meanwhile—funds of hedge funds run by experts who presumably possess an above-average ability to choose top hedge funds—was 9.4%, less than the S&P 500 return. And those numbers are pretax. Because hedge-fund and fund-of-fund fees are so high, the funds have to post much better gross returns than low-cost funds to deliver the same net return to investors.

But don't the world's smartest investors work at hedge funds? Don't they feast on the mistakes made by long-only mutual fund managers and individual investors? Some of them do, yes. But plenty of mutual fund managers and individual investors are brilliant, too. No matter how smart hedge fund managers are, moreover, they have to overcome a performance hurdle that others do not, namely the cost of their own vast compensation.

Most hedge funds charge 1%–2% of assets per year, plus 20% of gains (compared to most mutual funds, which don't charge success fees). These fees wallop net returns. Even if a hedge fund manager is skilled enough to beat the market by a few points before fees, in other words, investors won't necessarily see any benefit. Funds of funds, meanwhile, often charge 1% of assets and 10% of gains on top of the underlying hedge fund fees.

Average Annual Hedge Fund Returns, 1994–2004

	Return
Reported:	14.4%
LESS	

Survivorship bias:	2.4%
Incubation bias:	1.5%
Adjusted:	10.5%
S&P 500:	11%

Source: *Hedge Funds: An Industry in Its Adolescence*, William Fung and David Hsieh, 2006. Data from TASS database. Other hedge fund databases report slightly higher returns. S&P performance is from Ibbotson Associates.

For example, assume an S&P 500 index fund charges 0.2% of assets and generates a gross return of 10% a year, thus producing a net return of 9.8%. What gross return would a hedge fund charging the standard "two and twenty" (2% of assets and 20% of gains) have to generate to produce the same net return? *Fifteen* percent. The hedge fund's fees take such a big bite that the fund manager has to produce a gross return 50% better than the index fund's just to stay even. And a fund of funds? If a fund of funds takes another 1% and 10% on top of the hedge fund fees, it would have to generate a 19% gross return to equal the index fund's net.

Of course, all anyone really cares about are net returns, and if hedge fund managers are skilled enough to deliver positive returns when the market tanks, then it doesn't matter what they pay themselves. Before you wave off hedge fund costs as irrelevant, however, don't forget most hedge funds also come with a healthy dollop of the biggest cost of all: taxes.

Uncle Sam Loves Hedge Funds

The goal of most hedge funds is to make money now. This means trading at a pace that makes even hyperactive mutual fund managers seem patient. Hedge funds also avoid dividend-paying stocks because what makes money now is price appreciation. As a result, successful hedge funds often rack up mountains of short-term gains that, for taxable investors, create a huge tax load.

How much can short-term taxes eat into hedge-fund performance? Assume a hedge fund generates annual pretax net gains (after expenses) of 10% a year and that 75% of the gains come from short-term trading. With a 50% total tax liability (individual hedge fund investors are usually in the top tax bracket), and a 20% tax on the balance of the hedge fund's return, this would produce an after-tax return of just under 6%. At this rate, a $100,000 investment would appreciate to $405,000 after twenty-five years. This doesn't sound bad until you compare it to the after-tax performance of a mutual fund that generates the same 10% return through dividends and long-term gains. Assuming a 20% annual tax liability, the same $100,000 investment would produce an 8% after-tax return and grow to $685,000—more than twice as much.*

To generate the same *after-tax* wealth as a mutual fund, in other words, the hedge fund would have to generate an annual pretax return of 14% versus 10% for the long-term fund.**

---

*This calculation assumes, moreover, that the index fund *realizes* its long-term gains every year, which most don't. If the index fund does not realize most of its long-term gains until the end of the 25-year period (or until the fund holder sells the shares), the performance would be significantly better. If the fund holder eventually sells the fund, she will have to pay long-term capital gains taxes on as-yet-untaxed gain, but she will have enjoyed the benefit of compounding in the meantime. The tax difference between realized and unrealized long-term gains can be viewed as an interest-free loan from the government. You will eventually be on the hook for taxes on unrealized gains (unless you die), but in the meantime, you will enjoy the benefit of still having the cash compound in your account.

**Again, this calculation assumes that the hedge fund generates 75% of its return from realized short-term gains. If the fund harvests short-term

The bottom line? Pretax returns are not created equal, and tax inefficiency makes many hedge fund returns look much better than they really are.

When you put all the costs together—fees and taxes—you get a sense of just how skilled a hedge-fund manager has to be to generate *you,* the taxable investor, an above-market, after-tax return. Using the same fee and tax assumptions as above, to equal the net, after-tax return of an S&P 500 fund that generates a 10% gross return, a hedge fund would have to generate a gross return of no less than 20%. A fund of funds, meanwhile, would have to post a gross return of 24%. Few, if any, managers are skilled enough to produce such returns consistently.

Gross Returns Required for Same *After-tax* Net Return

	S&P 500 Fund	Hedge Fund	Fund of Funds
Gross Return:	10%	20%	24%
LESS			
Asset Fee	0.2%	2%	3%
Success Fee	—	20%	28%
Net Return	9.8%	14%	14%
LESS			
Taxes	20%	43%	43%
Net After-tax Return	7.8%	7.8%	7.8%

See Notes for description of tax and fee assumptions.

losses with which to offset realized gains or generates more return from dividends or long-term gains, the tax impact would be less. For example, a hedge fund that generated 50% of a 10% return from realized short-term gains and half from realized long-term gains would require a 12.5% gross return to match the net of the S&P 500 fund, instead of the 14% return in the example above.

More Risk Than You Think

As hedge fund returns have declined, the industry has begun emphasizing their diversification benefits. Most hedge funds are not closely "correlated" with the broader equity and bond markets, so the theory is that a well-chosen basket of hedge funds (or funds of funds) will reduce the risk of a diversified portfolio. According to recent academic research, however, the diversification benefits of hedge funds are overstated.

As described, the most common measure of investment risk is standard deviation: The amount each annual (or monthly) return varies around the average return. When hedge funds are examined using standard deviation, the risk/return profile does indeed seem impressive: hedge funds appear to generate returns with less-than-average risk. The trouble is that, unlike most mutual fund returns, most hedge fund returns are not normally distributed, so standard deviation does not tell the whole story. Specifically, hedge funds tend to display what academics call negative "skewness" and positive "kurtosis," which means that they have a greater-than-normal likelihood of generating extreme negative results.

The past performance of a hedge fund, in other words, can be *really* misleading. A mutual fund might slog along with quarterly returns that are accurately described by mean and standard deviation—e.g., GOOD, OKAY, GOOD, GOOD, FAIR, GOOD. With a hedge fund, however, the quarterly pattern might look like this: GOOD, GREAT, GREAT, GOOD, HORRIFIC.

According to professor Harry M. Kat of Cass Business School in London, moreover, the risk of extreme negative performance cannot be addressed by buying a basket of hedge funds—a strategy easily implemented by buying funds of funds. When one combines several funds in a portfolio (as a fund of funds does), Kat concludes, the standard deviation of the portfolio decreases (good), but the risk of an extreme negative outcome actually increases (bad). As the number of hedge funds in the portfolio increases, moreover, so does the basket's correlation with the overall stock market. This, in turn, reduces the diversification value of hedge funds.

If this sounds like a whole lot of academic mumbo jumbo—"If those profs really knew anything, they would be out there making billions instead of mewling from the ivory tower"*—then look at it this way. About 10% of hedge funds close their doors every year—a strategy employed more often when things have gone badly than when they have gone well—and only one-third have existed for more than five years.

The Best Business in the World

Of course, while the secret that hedge funds can make you money in bear markets was spreading among investors, another secret was spreading among professional money managers: hedge funds can make you *a fortune in any market*. Before this revelation, it seemed that mutual funds were the greatest game in town. After the compensation packages of a few hedge fund managers became common knowledge, however, mutual fund pay seemed like chicken feed. Why

---

*Many academics actually *are* practicing what they preach. Jeremy Siegel of Wharton is a senior advisor to WisdomTree, an index fund firm. Burton Malkiel, a Princeton professor and the author of *A Random Walk Down Wall Street,* was a director at Vanguard. Eugene Fama of the University of Chicago and Kenneth French of Dartmouth are senior advisors at Dimensional Fund Advisors, one of the most successful fund firms.

make a measly 1% a year when you can make 1%–2% plus 20% of gains? Why, indeed. And, so, everyone and his brother started a hedge fund.

But aren't those massive hedge-fund pay packages just compensation for higher risk? Isn't working for a hedge fund riskier than working for a mutual fund? Don't hedge fund managers deserve to get paid for the value they generate?

Sort of. Hedge fund managers, like most capitalists, deserve to get paid whatever the market will bear (in this case, an absolutely dizzying amount). Working for a five-person hedge fund start-up is indeed riskier than working at, say, Fidelity or Colgate-Palmolive, and, unlike many mutual fund managers, hedge fund managers usually do tie their fees to performance. But the concepts of "risk" and "performance-based compensation" in the hedge-fund business are relative. If a hedge fund folds, its analysts and portfolio managers can usually find new jobs at other hedge funds (or they can just change the name on the door and start a new fund). In the meantime, even if the hedge fund never generates a profit, the managers can take home the same 1%–2% of assets that supports the average mutual fund in perpetuity. In other words, a hedge fund manager's "risk" is not that she will starve but that she won't make a killing. There are riskier pursuits in life.

And then, of course, there is the definition of "profit." If the stock market tanks, few investors would resent paying a hedge fund manager 20% of a gain. If the market soars, however, and a long/short equity hedge fund soars with it, has the hedge fund really made a profit? Shouldn't the "profit" just be the amount over and above the underlying market return? Arguably, yes. In most cases, however, the hedge fund gets paid for the whole absolute gain, regardless of what the market does.

The good news is that academics have recently begun to isolate the passive market factors that drive most hedge fund returns, the same way they have isolated the factors that produce most stock market returns. As the conclusions become more accepted, sophisticated investors should be able to benchmark hedge fund returns more effectively, and pay managers only for manager-generated *alpha*, rather than market-generated *beta*. Eventually, Wall Street will also probably develop passive funds based on the major hedge fund strategies, which should allow small investors to take advantage of their diversification benefits without today's costs and risks.*

In the meantime, remember this: The "risk" of hedge funds is far greater for hedge fund *investors* than hedge fund managers, and this risk is bigger than you might think. As with the best mutual funds, the *best* hedge funds have delivered extraordinary risk-adjusted returns. As with mutual funds, however, to have identified these funds in advance would have required what one professor deems "supernatural" fund-picking talent. And the point of investing intelligently is to avoid needing occult help to succeed.

---

*Such funds will be different from today's "hedge fund index" products, which invest in hedge funds and then layer on another layer of fees. A better hedge fund index fund would isolate the market factors that drive the returns of a particular hedge-fund strategy and invest directly in the underlying securities. Such funds would not charge "two and twenty." Instead, their fees would resemble those of today's long-only passive funds.

16

Investment Research

If you are committed to playing the stock picking game—which, after reading this book, I hope you won't be—you will probably use research: Company research, stock research, industry research, currency research, quantitative research, technical research, economic research and/or asset allocation research. The research might be produced by any number of sources: Brokerage firms, banks, consulting firms, independent research firms, universities, individuals, news organizations, blogs or publishing companies. It might be distributed for free or cost you an arm and a leg. It might be written by world-renowned investment gurus or anonymous no-names. It might be insightful, defensible and unique—or flimsy, derivative and asinine (and you might or might not be able to tell the difference).

In any event, if you use research, remember this: There are only two ways that it can help you beat the market. Either by 1) telling you something important that the majority of investors don't yet know, or 2) triggering an insight that the majority of investors don't yet have.

After the research scandals a few years ago, the common wisdom was that research produced by brokerage firms was worthless and that research produced by independent firms was great. This was silly. Research quality varies regardless of what type of firm produces it: Some is garbage, most is average and some is outstanding. Unfortunately, unless you have a deep grounding in the subject matter of a particular report, your ability to evaluate its quality will be limited. On even the most common questions—"What is the market going to do next year?" "What is such-and-such a stock worth?"—analysts use dozens of metrics, methodologies, theories and conventions, many of which are flawed or misused. The devil is in the details (usually the assumptions), and you often have to be an expert to know which conclusions are valid and why.

In terms of research telling you something most investors don't know, small firms do have an advantage because their distribution is usually limited. The big weakness of most brokerage-firm research is that *everyone has it.* By the time you read a brokerage research report, any new information or insights it contains will already have been read and acted on by thousands of institutional investors (who received phone summaries seconds after it was published), and, therefore, will already have been factored into market prices.

The way investment research is most likely to help you, therefore, is by helping you develop to an insight that the majority of investors don't have. Such an insight might match the opinion articulated in the report (an opinion that, for whatever reason, the majority of investors disagree with), or it might be the opposite. Regardless, if the insight is valuable, you will likely develop it after consuming *multiple* research reports, along with financial statements, conference call transcripts, company presentations, customer comments, news stories and other inputs—a "mosaic" of information to which each research report may make only a small contribution.

Whatever you do, don't make an investment decision just because a particular analyst or "guru" recommends it. Even the best analysts are often wrong. Also remember that, just as most investors lag the market, most *analysts* would lag the market if they actually had to put their ideas into practice. When an analyst demonstrates irrefutable stock picking talent, one of two things happens: Either she goes to work for a hedge fund (where she can make orders of magnitude more money) or her pronouncements become so widely followed that they no longer help you gain an edge.

In the active-trading game, there's only one analyst's opinion that matters: Yours. Since high-quality research can help you develop and refine your opinions, however, and since you will be bombarded by research of *all* qualities regardless, it helps to know more about it.

What "Buy" Means

When a brokerage analyst rates a stock "buy," is he or she advising you to buy it? Actually, no. In most cases, a "buy" rating—or, for that matter, a "sell," "hold," "outperform," "accumulate" or other rating—is not intended to advise you, a specific investor with specific goals, circumstances and requirements, to do anything. Why not? Because *an analyst is not a financial advisor*. Analyzing a security is less than half the work required to give investment advice. An analyst can form an opinion about the outlook for a security. The analyst cannot, however, make a judgment about whether you should buy or sell it.

Any investment decision, in other words, involves at least two analyses: 1) an analysis of the stock, fund, etc., and 2) an analysis of the goals, risk tolerance, investment style, time horizon and portfolio composition of the investor. In most cases, the decision also involves analyses of asset classes (stocks, bonds, etc.) relative industry attractiveness (technology vs. healthcare, etc.) and other stocks in the sector (if you're going to buy one semiconductor stock, is this the right one?). At most brokerage firms, these analyses are conducted by different professionals: the stock analyst, the portfolio strategist and the financial advisor. Without knowing the circumstances and requirements of particular investors, a stock analyst cannot make action recommendations.

So why do firms use ratings like "buy," "sell" and "hold?" Most firms actually don't, anymore (nothing like outrage and lawsuits to motivate clarity). Firms that do use "buy" and "sell" ratings, meanwhile, are usually just following a time-honored Wall Street tradition. From time immemorial, investors have referred to stocks they like as "buys" and stocks they hate as "sells." Most firms also explain that ratings are *not* action recommendations—in clear language that no one reads. Even when firms don't use the word "buy," they are often described as employing an "equivalent of buy," so the change of terms doesn't help much.

Lest this sound wishy-washy—"Why can't they just tell me what to do?"—consider the role of the sector analyst in the investment process. Responsible investing does not start with industry-specific stock picking. Responsible investing starts with asset-level diversification (the percentages of a portfolio that one places in stocks, bonds, cash, etc.). It then moves through multiple decisions, many of which can be executed using passive funds: market allocation (United States, international, emerging markets); industry allocation (broad, sector specific, etc.); investment style selection (active, passive, value, growth, etc.); and fund and security selection. Even for active managers, stock-picking is the last decision in the hierarchy, and the least important. Picking the wrong stock in a well-diversified portfolio is merely annoying. Making the wrong asset allocation decision can be devastating.

Stock research, therefore, should be used only at the end of the investment process, and only to help answer questions like "Which stocks in this industry might do better than others?" and "How well might they do?" These questions are of greatest importance to professional investors, who can beat benchmarks only through superior stock picking. For most individual investors, the questions are, or should be, irrelevant.

Another problem with ratings is that one investor's "buy" is always another's "sell." When Google went public, it was a high-risk stock. Before considering the outlook for the security, therefore, Google was a "buy" for only a small percentage of investors. Ratings also mean different things at different firms. Some rating systems are "absolute": The analyst must judge whether the stock will go up or down a certain amount over a certain period. Other systems are "relative": The analyst must judge whether the stock will do better or worse than a market or industry benchmark. In a "relative" system, a stock rated "buy" might actually be expected to drop in price.

The point is that the responsibilities of stock analysts, who assess the outlook for a handful of stocks in a single industry, are different than those of financial advisors, who develop investment advice for specific clients. Single-word stock ratings convey only a fraction of the information necessary to make an investment decision. So don't buy a stock just because an analyst rates it "buy."

Why Wall Street Hates the "S" Word

While we're on the subject of ratings, we might as well clear up a mystery: Why there are so few "sell" ratings. During the research scandals, the paucity of "sells" was cited as proof of corruption: analysts allegedly knew stocks were headed into the tank but published "buy" ratings just to butter up investment-banking clients. So regulators restructured the industry, skewered alleged miscreants (yours truly), and steered hundreds of millions of dollars to independent research firms. And two years after the delousing, were half of stocks rated "sell"?

Nope.

At the end of 2004, American Technology Research, one of the new breed of independents—a firm "dedicated to delivering quality, unbiased, fundamental research"—rated a whopping 4% of stocks it covered "sell." Other firms had similar percentages.

So, what's the real reason there are so few "sells"? To begin with, there is selection bias. Wall Street analysts don't usually cover all the stocks in an industry, or even the majority. Why not? Because it doesn't make financial sense. Covering a stock costs time and money, and brokerage firms are not nonprofit organizations.* Brokerage firms don't make money by selling stock research or picking stocks. They make money by selling investment banking services to companies and advice to investors. As a result, brokerage firms tend to cover 1) the stocks of companies that do a lot of banking business, and

---

*A typical research team, composed of one senior analyst ($1 million a year) and two junior analysts ($200,000 a year, each), can cover about 10–20 stocks. Throw in another $200,000 of overhead, travel and other expenses, and covering a stock costs about $80,000–$160,000 per year.

2) stocks that lots of investors care about. The latter category includes large, widely owned stocks and small but heavily traded stocks. The stocks that Wall Street analysts cover, in other words, will not be the stocks likely to go up the most at any given time.

Selection bias also leads firms to cover stocks they believe have favorable prospects instead of stocks that don't (i.e., "buys" instead of "sells"). Most of the cost in covering a stock is up front, and if an analyst thinks a company's future is dim, the incentive to incur this cost is limited. Also, most investors are "long only," meaning that they can only own stocks, they can't sell them short (a way of betting the price will drop). Consequently, most investors don't want or need to hear about dogs.

Next, analysts are subject to the usual human tendencies, such as herding: When the majority of analysts are bullish, a bear may think he is missing something. And, yes, it is true that when the crowd is optimistic (and right), being pessimistic can be risky to an analyst's livelihood.

The research scandal focused on one potential source of research conflict—investment banking—but ignored the other two: companies *and* investors. Even with strict disclosure rules, the most valuable commodity on Wall Street is information, and relationships still matter. A press release can't convey a CEO's facial expression when he or she is startled by a pointed question—and such expressions can transmit more information than a 100-page SEC filing. The top analysts, therefore, spend years cultivating relationships with company managers, and these can evaporate in an instant when the analyst goes negative. The first time I downgraded a stock other analysts loved, for example, the company's management shut me out for months, hampering my ability to do my job. Although such blatant retribution is rarer now, companies still exact revenge. One of the most valuable services brokerage firms provide for big investors, for example, is arranging for company managers to visit their offices. Many companies refuse to do this for firms whose analysts are negative on their stocks.

Investors, too, carry big sticks, and they don't hesitate to swing them. Major fund companies pay the Street hundreds of millions of dollars a year—way more than even the biggest banking clients. When a fund company owns, say, 5% of GE, and an influential brokerage-firm analyst trashes the stock, the fund managers don't usually call the firm and say, "Thanks for the tip." They do call, but they usually say something along the lines of, "Your analyst is an idiot, and thanks to his big mouth, we are getting creamed." An analyst who routinely takes potshots at sacred-cow stocks won't be regarded as helpful for long, especially if he or she is wrong. (If the analyst is right, that's a different story, but the institutions have analysts, too, and if they thought the brokerage analyst was right, they wouldn't own the stock.)

A final contributor to the predominance of "buy" ratings requires some historical perspective. As Warren Buffett has observed, most investors make decisions based on the "rearview mirror": Specifically, they expect more in the future of what they have seen in the *recent* past. In 2000, when fewer than 1% of stocks were rated "sell," the market had been rising for eighteen years. Analysts, investors, brokers and commentators under forty had experienced nothing but a bull market, and many of those over forty had either left the industry or concluded that the nasty 1970s were, thankfully, ancient history.

As we know, long bull markets breed optimism: Investors are far more bullish at the end of them than at the beginning.

The happy memories of 1982 to 1999 remain fresh, and most analysts and investors still expect a return to this trend. In ten years, if the market has remained stagnant, investors and analysts will gradually get more bearish, and the percentage of "sell" ratings should finally increase.

Playing the Odds

There is yet another reason why Wall Street is usually bullish, one that should help you keep the opinion of any analyst in perspective. Remember how easy it is to mistake luck for skill in the markets? Well, this works two ways. One lesson all Wall Street analysts learn early in their careers, usually through the sting of public humiliation, is that it's better to be right for the wrong reasons than wrong. The way to be right more often than not is to play the odds. And so, consciously or unconsciously, most Wall Street analysts do.

For example, right now, Wall Street strategists are updating their predictions for the current year and offering them for next. (They're always doing this.) They are analyzing interest rates, valuation, profits, economic policies, geopolitics, sentiment, technical and quantitative metrics, and dozens of other factors. And, as usual, most of them are predicting that the market is going to go . . . up.

Which is understandable. Because the market usually does go up. If not for the reasons that the strategists predict, well, then, just because it usually goes up. From 1872 to 2005, according to data compiled by Yale's Robert Shiller, the S&P 500 has risen in eighty-five out of 134 years (63%) and fallen in forty-nine (37%). Strategists who predicted the market would rise every year, in other words—regardless of the logic used—

would have been right nearly two-thirds of the time. In the investing business, you can make a lot of money and acquire an excellent reputation if you are right two-thirds of the time.

But this, again, is why market forecasting is different from, say, astrology or tarot card reading: In the markets, the future is not unlimited—it is binary. Stocks and markets can only go up or down. And this, in turn, is why thousands of professionals and millions of amateurs who are perceived as having forecasting skill may, in fact, have no more than a Halloween-party swami with a turban and crystal ball.

Because stocks and markets can only go up or down, market forecasters usually have at least fifty-fifty odds of being "right." Because the stock market is not random, moreover, but loosely tracks the growth of profits and dividends, forecasters who predict the market is going to rise have better than fifty-fifty odds (over time, profits and dividends usually increase). In the latest bull market, from 1982 to 2000, the market went up in fifteen of eighteen years, so bearish analysts and strategists were almost always wrong. Even in long-term bear markets, the odds favor being bullish. In any given year, the market is just as likely to go up as to go down.

Here's the catch, though. Human psychology being what it is, stock forecasters—and those who evaluate them—almost never factor these odds into their assessments of the forecasters' skills. When I put a $400 target on Amazon, for example, some observers reacted with shock, as though the odds against this were 1,000-to-1. I personally put the odds at slightly better than even. (Of course, with these odds, the Amazon call wouldn't have been as compelling a story: "He predicted 'heads,' and it came up . . . 'HEADS!' Ladies and gentlemen, we have a *guru*.")

Similarly, those who buy stocks that go up often forget that they had fifty-fifty odds. Instead, they congratulate themselves on their acumen and make a bigger bet next time. In a bull market, when the odds are so good that it's hard to be wrong, most people come to believe that the next investing bestseller should be titled *George Soros, Warren Buffett and Me*. Most people, in other words, let bull market success go to their heads.

If you want to keep your money, don't let this happen: It is the bull market that is making you rich, not you. Similarly, don't let *someone else's* bull market success go to your head. Beware all investing gurus, especially self-appointed ones. No matter how smart the gurus may seem, no matter how much other people respect them, the gurus *do not know* what the market is going to do. True gurus—Warren Buffett, for example—freely admit this. Unfortunately, their candor only leads people to place even more trust and faith in them. Then, when the predictions are wrong, people blame the gurus: "How dare you con me into trusting you!" Don't blame the gurus. They are not Nostradamuses, and if they have an ounce of self-awareness and humility, they will not claim to be. Instead, like Bill Miller, the Legg Mason portfolio manager who recently beat the S&P 500 for fifteen years in a row, they will know how important a role luck can play.

Again, this is not to say that all investing success is luck. It isn't. Some people—Bill Miller and Warren Buffett, for example—are skilled, and, over time, some do generate superior returns. This skill, however, has little to do with the simplistic price predictions that dominate most market discourse. It stems from discipline, patience, experience and methodologies that lead to a rare ability to determine when the odds are distinctly good or bad. Skilled investors aren't immune from mistakes. They are just talented enough that eventually, gradually, their better odds allow them to win.

What Stock Analysts Are Good For

If few forecasting tools can reliably predict what stocks are going to do, if the vast majority of stock pickers subtract value, and if the best strategy for most people is to invest in low-cost index funds, then what the heck are stock analysts for? Why are thousands of analysts paid millions of dollars to do work that, on average, apparently isn't worth the cost of the chairs they sit on?

The answer is complex. To begin with, it turns out that stock analysts are valuable—sometimes very valuable—but not in the way that most of the public and press think. Specifically, casual observers view analysts simply as "stock pickers," when stock picking is actually one of the least helpful services they provide. An analyst whose only goal was to pick the best stocks in the market would not confine the search to a single industry or waste time writing reports about company or industry fundamentals. Instead, he or she would constantly screen thousands of stocks to find the few with the most promising characteristics. Most analysts function more like beat reporters: They follow handfuls of stocks in narrow industry sectors and try to form opinions about each of them.

A brokerage analyst's goal, furthermore, is to help the firm's clients make better decisions, a mission that includes doing much more than assessing the prospects of stocks. As described, a "buy" for one client will always be a "sell" for another, so even if an analyst were the greatest forecaster in the world, he would have to rate stocks differently depending on which clients he was talking to. Also, on Wall Street, opinions are a dime a dozen, but cogent, persuasive arguments are rare. As a result, the value in what a strong analyst has to say lies in *why* he thinks what he thinks, not just *what* he thinks.

To understand the value unrelated to stock picking that an analyst can provide, it helps to look at a few examples. Back in the dot-com days, for instance, when grocery-delivery company Webvan was going to revolutionize food shopping, the company's executives assured investors that their trucks could make four to six deliveries an hour. This seemed plausible—until an analyst named Mark Rowen rented a car, followed a few trucks around, and reported that they could only make two to three deliveries per hour (one of many reasons the company went bust). The same year, when hedge funds were salivating for insight into Amazon's performance in the critical holiday season, an analyst named Jamie Kiggen temporarily traded his suit for a temp job at one of the company's distribution centers. After loading thousands of packages onto conveyor belts, Kiggen quit moonlighting, took the train back to Wall Street, and reported that morale was high and business strong. When you are managing a big portfolio—or trading from home—you don't have time to hit the road to see whether management is full of it. If you read Rowen and Kiggen's research, you didn't have to.

On a more mundane level, most of what analysts do consists of scrutinizing financial filings, interviewing company managers to understand business subtleties or quirks in financial statements, interviewing vendors and customers, tracking industry data, attending conferences, talking to investors and industry experts and shaping mountains of raw data into financial and industry forecasts—all with the aim of helping investors make better-informed decisions. Most investors follow multiple industries and hundreds of stocks, so the time they can devote to tracking a single sector is limited. If nothing else, therefore, a strong sector analyst can save them time.

The work of a great analyst, of course, will go beyond this. A great analyst will not only gather, organize, and assess relevant information and trends, but will also make bold arguments that challenge conventional views. Doing this is risky—the analyst will be unpopular (initially), and his or her reputation will be on the line—but it is the most valuable service an analyst can provide. Even if the analyst's arguments are wrong, they can help investors confront ideas and data they might otherwise have failed to consider. While taking stands does involve stock predictions, it is not "stock-picking," per se. The analyst is not surveying 7,000 stocks to find the most promising, or even trying to find the one stock in an industry that will make investors the most money. Instead, the analyst is attacking a consensus position and possibly upending it, thus improving the efficiency of the market as a whole.

Which brings us back to the original question: If, despite all these efforts, the market is so hard to beat, why have analysts at all? The simple answer—a tautological one—is that as long as there are investors who try to beat the market, there will be analysts who try to help them.

The more profound answer is that one of the reasons the market is so hard to beat, even for professionals, is that, in aggregate, analysts and investors are good at what they do (evaluating, distributing, and wringing the profit out of every piece of information). After an eighteen-year bull market, the number of analysts ballooned beyond what was needed to get the job done, but Wall Street is nothing if not laser-focused on the bottom line. Over time, if the market stays stagnant, many analysts will eventually leave the profession. But there will always be jobs for the best of them.

Summary

The intelligent way to employ investment research is to use it to understand and analyze the smart arguments on both sides of an issue—and then decide for yourself. No analyst knows what is right for you, and even the best ones are often wrong. Clear-headed research can help you develop, refine and test your own conclusions. If you don't feel comfortable making your own conclusions, or if you just want someone to tell you what to do, you shouldn't use investment research at all.

17

The Investment Media

And now we turn to the biases and hazards of the investment media, the filter through which Wall Street is usually viewed.

Let's start with the positive: The press plays a vital role on Wall Street. It polices and exposes sleazy practices, informs and educates investors, and generally offers a mind-boggling amount of information and commentary at a very low price. Without the investment media, Wall Street would be even more dangerous to the uninitiated than it already is, and many practices deserving of reform would never be noticed. Fascinating debates about the direction of markets, economies, commodity prices, interest rates and house prices, would be confined to professional circles. We would not benefit from the insights of smart columnists like Jonathan Clements of the *Wall Street Journal* and Jason Zweig of *Money* magazine, along with dozens of smart CNBC guests, op-ed contributors and investment journalists. We would, perhaps, be even less aware of the devastating mistakes most investors make than we already are.

Of course, there's no free lunch, and as we feast on gripping stories of past and future price moves, dueling predictions, and conflicts of interest, we should keep in mind that the investment media's interests are quite different from our own. How? To stay in business, the investment media must persuade us to read, watch, or listen. Why does this matter? Because intelligent investing is about as riveting as watching bread rise.

The way for the investment media to succeed is to grab your attention and tell you something you *absolutely need to know*. The way for *you* to succeed, meanwhile, is to allocate your assets, reduce your costs, and then understand that there is almost *nothing* that you absolutely need to know. To make matters worse (for the media), intelligent investing has nothing in common with the other time-tested attention-grabbing device: a good story. Good stories are driven by drama, character, color, action, controversy, protagonists, and change. Intelligent investment returns, meanwhile, are driven by inaction, patience, and time.

Markets will crash; markets will soar. Googles and eBays will blast off; Enrons and WorldComs will crater. Some people will get rich; others will get frog-marched to jail. The stories will be captivating, outrageous, nauseating—you won't be able to turn them off or put them down. As far as intelligent investing is concerned, however, they are just noise.

Still, the investment media must keep you watching, listening, and reading, or else they—not you, they—will go bankrupt. How will they do this? They will just suggest, over and over again, that there are exciting new places to put your money or dangerous places to remove it from. (Possibly true, but transaction costs, taxes and market-timing mistakes will kill you.) They will tantalize you with the latest, greatest mutual funds or the "Ten Hot Stocks for 2007." (If it were that easy to identify the "ten hot stocks" every mutual fund in the

Top Ten Rules of Investment Media Self-Defense

- As far as your own investments go, ignore 97% of what you hear, see, and read
- Remember that market cycles and news cycles operate in different time frames (thirty to forty years for the former; thirty to forty *hours* for the latter)
- Remember that, for the investment media to survive, they must keep you watching, reading and listening
- Remember that the media must focus on what has changed, what is changing and what will change ("news")—and that the rules of intelligent investing almost never change
- Draw a sharp distinction between investing and entertainment
- Remember that you will want to buy funds, stocks, markets, and the like that are lauded by the media, but that the media does not actually know what these funds, stocks and markets will do
- Remember that many of the world's smartest investors would not be caught dead appearing on CNBC or in the *Wall Street Journal*
- Remember that those who *do* appear on CNBC or in the *Journal* may well have an agenda
- Remember that reporters, editors, producers and anchors *always* have an agenda: to get you to watch, read or listen

country would already have bought them.) They will make you drool by observing, again and again, that every dollar invested in Microsoft's IPO in 1986 would be worth hundreds of dollars today. (So? Everything's obvious in hindsight.) They will forever detail new ways to pick winners, beat the pros or make millions. (Noble goals, but hard to achieve).

Such stories are gripping, but their implicit message—"Do something!"—is hazardous. Once you have gotten the investing basics right, you should do almost nothing. Every time you make a change, you incur costs and decrease your odds of success. The least predictable investment decisions are those focused on the short term, whereas the most predictable are those focused on the long term. But for the investment media the long term is death. How often will you tune in to be told that you shouldn't do anything different, that nothing has changed? Never. So the investment media will find other ways to keep you entertained.

They will tell you what the markets have done and what they might do (*interesting, but irrelevant*). They will tell you which stocks are hot and which stocks are not (*interesting, irrelevant*). They will stage bull-bear debates (*interesting, irrelevant*). They will worship those who have been right lately and trash those who have been wrong (*interesting but misleading: Those who have been right lately are no more likely to be right in the future*). They will trot out an endless supply of tools and statistics you might use to whip the market (*interesting, usually irrelevant*). They will pounce on the latest scandal, swindle or fraud as shocking evidence that the world is going to hell in a handbasket—and that it might take you with it (*fraud has been with us since the dawn of time, as have bankruptcies and market crashes*). They will pander to you, by blaming your losses on everyone but you. (It was someone else's fault!) They will promise to divulge the secrets of "insiders" (*there really aren't any "insiders," at least not any who know what the market is going to do*). They will encourage, forever, the part of you that wants to believe that, by watching this show, reading this research, following this guru, avoiding this mistake or pursuing this strategy, you, too, can strike it rich (*unlikely*).

The investment media are extraordinarily good at what they do. If you get in the habit of reading news wires, watching CNBC, and obsessively checking Yahoo! Finance, you will find that this comes to feel as necessary as breathing. You will know the arguments and action of the day, recognize the major players, and feel the market excitement. You will develop strong opinions about the future. You will feel like an integral member of a global community, the investment community, and you will soon note that almost *no one* in this community mentions topics like passive investing, transaction costs, standard deviation, investment policy or time horizons longer than a few months. You will infer that the intelligent way to invest is the way all the intelligent people in your community invest—actively. If you aren't careful, you will eventually forget that there is a difference between investing and entertainment.

Careful!

Read, watch and listen all you want, because there is no more fascinating, dynamic and surprising show in the world. But never forget that intelligent investing has *nothing* to do with the daily market show. You can't learn to hit a forehand like Roger Federer by reading a tennis magazine. And you can't learn to invest like Warren Buffett by reading a newspaper or watching TV.

A few years ago, when it was fashionable to associate one's business with all the money being made in the stock market, the slogan of the most popular financial TV network, CNBC, was "Profit From It." If your definition of "profiting from it" was loose enough to include "being entertained," the network could, indeed, have made you rich. If your definition was making more money, however, you would have been better off turning off the TV and getting back to work. A similar strategy, unfortunately, makes sense with most investment commentary.

A Cautionary Tale of Market Wizards

Before we leave the world of professionals and move onto the greatest Wall Street danger of all (you), it's time for some stories. The stories illustrate many of the themes I have been hammering on: the danger of focusing on short-term returns; the limits of valuation as a price prediction tool; the difficulty of market timing; the temptation to chase past performance; the influence of the press; the shortcomings of even the most talented professionals; and the ever-present tug-of-war between investment risk and business risk, in which investment principles are forever balanced with the day-to-day realities of competition, clients and commerce.

The stories are from the bubble years, but their lessons are still relevant. The protagonists, moreover, are not your average clock-punching mutual fund managers or twenty-four-year-old hedge-fund analysts—folks who, from apathy or inexperience, might be expected to make amateur mistakes. Rather, they are men who are (or were) the Michael Jordans of the investing world.

Let's begin in 1995, in Boston, at one of the largest and most respected financial firms on the planet: Fidelity. At the end of 1995, the star portfolio manager of the country's biggest mutual fund, Magellan, turned cautious on the stock market. The manager, Jeff Vinik, had bet heavily on technology stocks in the preceding two years—and made a killing doing so. In late 1995, however, with the market's valuation approaching that of previous bull-market peaks, Vinik concluded that "stocks appeared historically overvalued relative to bonds," and that "there was considerable speculation in the stock market overall," especially in technology. So, he dumped his tech stocks and shifted a third of Magellan's assets into cash and Treasury bonds.

As Fidelity would soon scramble to point out, Jeff Vinik was no rookie. In the three years he had run Magellan, he had racked up an average gain of nearly 20% a year, well ahead of the S&P 500, and he had also beaten the market in his previous Fidelity assignments. His cautious move, therefore, wasn't the impulsive swap of a young trader or the schizoid lurch of a Captain Queeg. On the contrary, it was a defensible and conservative decision given what Vinik knew at the time. Had the market and tech stocks actually gone south, with Magellan safely rid of them, one can only imagine the cheers that would have rained down on him and Fidelity. But they didn't.

Three months later, with Magellan up for the year but lagging the S&P by a few percentage points, Vinik (and Fidelity and Magellan) were getting bloodied from coast to coast. Vinik's "timing could not have been much worse," the *Los Angeles Times* chided, in a typical article. His "decision to load up on bonds has made Magellan. . . one of the worst performers this year." Despite the torrent of money flowing into mutual funds in those days, Magellan's inflows reversed, as impatient shareholders headed for the doors: "Magellan's dismal performance . . . ," the *Wall Street Journal* later reported, "cost it an estimated $5 billion or more of net redemptions." Magellan's fees—and Jeff Vinik's compensation—were based, in part, on the fund's performance relative to the market. No wonder, then, that by early May, only six months after Vinik lightened up on stocks, "speculation on Wall Street [was] rampant about whether Fidelity [would] replace Mr. Vinik at the helm of Magellan." Whether Fidelity did boot Vinik—or whether he just got sick of the media battering and quit—was never publicly explained. In any case, shortly thereafter, he left the firm.*

Magellan was the largest mutual fund in the country, so perhaps the scrutiny was understandable. This said, it is telling to review the kind of decision (soon deemed a "risky bet") that led to months of bad press, billions of dollars of shareholder redemptions, and, ultimately, the end of Vinik's Fidelity career. In late 1995, the U.S. economy was still going strong, but, concerned that stock valuations had gotten too high—and aware that, by the time an economic or market downturn is obvious, it's too late—Vinik had reduced Magellan's equity exposure. He hadn't turned chicken, by any means: Magellan kept two-thirds of its assets in stocks. He also hadn't lost money: Vinik's "dismal returns" consisted of being up 2.4% for the first four months of 1996. He had, however, lagged the market for a few months, and now he was gone.

Vinik's experiences served as a warning beacon for other fund managers: lag your benchmark, and you'll be history. The real risk for money managers, in other words, was (and is) not losing money, but straying from the benchmark. If the market dropped and your fund lost money, you could blame the market and hide in the crowd. If the market soared,

*Vinik's story ended happily: He founded his own hedge fund and, sheltered from the media scrutiny, delivered extraordinary returns over the next several years.

however, and your fund lagged behind? Well, then you were screwed.

From a business- and career-risk perspective, in other words, absolute performance was less important than where the fund placed in the rankings of the fund rating organizations, Lipper and Morningstar. The fund rankings were updated not yearly, but *weekly*, and even if portfolio managers managed to ignore them, their customers, bosses, and the financial press did not. As the decade progressed, and the mutual fund business got ever more competitive (and profitable), the focus on the relative rankings intensified. One exasperated portfolio manager told me that, by 1999, his boss was sending him an e-mail every Thursday analyzing his relative performance for the prior five days.

Jeff Vinik's caution in 1996, as it turned out, was severely premature. Over the next three years, the major market indices more than doubled. Time and again, those who predicted that the bull market had run its course looked alarmist—and stupid. And time and again, they were rewarded for their pessimism by being relieved of their reputations and jobs.

The turn of the millennium did not ease the pressure on money managers to keep up with competitors, nor the incentive for the press to highlight fallen stars. *Institutional Investor,* a magazine that might be expected to have a deeper understanding of wise investment policy than the average publication, kicked off 2000 by highlighting the woes of the most celebrated investor of our time—an international icon whose 1999 had yielded the almost comically pitiful gain of one-half of one percent (when NASDAQ was up 86%). The investor had not only missed the tech stock boom, the magazine chided, he was also "underinvested in equities." The article stressed that the investor was "in no danger of losing his status as a legend," but the headline said it all: "Warren Buffetted."

If Warren Buffett was in no danger of losing his status as a legend, he was about the only one who wasn't. One by one, erstwhile gurus had been carried out on stretchers. UBS's Gary Brinson. Fidelity's George Vanderheiden. Oakmark's Robert Sanborn. All had earned extraordinary returns for years. All had apparently lost their touch. Even those who left of their own volition had had doors slammed behind them. Chuck Clough, a renowned Merrill Lynch strategist who had turned cautious on the equity market in 1998, quit in mid–1999 because he wanted to start his own firm. The *Wall Street Journal* bid him farewell by suggesting that the real reason he had left was that he had committed Wall Street's "cardinal sin: being bearish, and wrong." What the article did not mention—or even contemplate—was that Clough was not wrong, but *early*.

Nor was the job-and-reputation destruction limited to mere all-stars. For years, the two archetypal hedge funds had been Julian Robertson's Tiger Management and George Soros's Soros Fund Management. Such was the mystique of these firms that when Tiger or Soros wanted to meet with me, I felt as though John McEnroe had asked for some help with his serve. With Tiger, especially, the meetings were memorable because of the rare combination of ferocity and grace of the man at the helm. A North Carolina native, the sixty-seven-year-old Julian Robertson could swear politely. In an age of business-casual, in which power and wealth often correlated inversely with the cost of one's clothes, Robertson once apologized profusely for not wearing his suit jacket when greeting me at his office door.

A diehard value shop, Tiger yearned to short the Internet stocks—and reportedly had, with disastrous results. One of

Julian's favorite targets was Amazon, and whenever he was itching to give it another go, he would call me to see what the bulls were thinking. I would ramble on about returns on capital, negative operating cycles and revenue momentum, and Julian would listen for as long as he could stand it. Then, his voice roaring off the glass walls of the office, he would envelope me in that North Carolina drawl:

"Well, Henry, that's just ridiculous. How can people pay these prices? For a *bookstore*!"

From 1980 through 1997, Tiger's funds had beaten the market by a phenomenal margin, returning about 30% per year. By early 1998, after seventeen years of spectacular performance, the firm's assets under management peaked at nearly $23 billion, a gargantuan sum. Then technology stocks really took off. Tiger lost money in 1998 and got crushed in 1999. In his 1999 letter to shareholders, Julian was characteristically direct: "These results stink." His forthrightness and amazing record, however, did not stop clients from withdrawing money by the billions. And the returns just got worse. By the end of March 2000, when Julian finally threw in the towel, his funds were down another 14% for the year. It had taken Tiger more than fifteen years to grow its assets to $23 billion. Thanks to redemptions and losses, however, the assets shrank to $6 billion in only two years.

Those best equipped to comment on the fall of legends are other legends. For color on Tiger's demise, therefore, the *New York Times* turned to Stan Druckenmiller, the chief investment officer and second-in-command at Soros Fund Management, the largest hedge fund complex in the world. "It's not a sad day," Druckenmiller reportedly said, referring to Julian's departure. "It's like a guy who double-bogeys the last holes but still wins the golf tournament; he has a phenomenal record."

Druckenmiller was talking about Robertson, but he might as well have been talking about himself. A month later—for the same reason—he, too, would be out of a job.

In a market dominated by a single red-hot strategy (in this case, growth and technology stocks), fund managers have two options: They can bet against the trend, as Julian did, and pray that it turns before they get demolished, or they can play along, as Druckenmiller did, and pray that they get *out* before they get demolished. For those tempted to conclude that Julian's mistake was stubbornness, Druckenmiller's experience illustrates that the opposite approach isn't necessarily any better.

When technology stocks took off, Druckenmiller, like Robertson, got kicked in the teeth. Unlike Robertson, however, Druckenmiller didn't blame the market—he rolled with it. In the summer of 1999, with Soros's Quantum Fund down nearly 20% for the year, Druckenmiller reversed course and loaded up on technology stocks. Quantum staged a spectacular rally, finishing up 35% for the year, and Druckenmiller again, briefly, looked like the market wizard he was. "If someone wants to say we're joining the momentum guys, that's fine," the *Wall Street Journal* quoted him as saying. "It's our job to figure out how to make money."

The plunge into technology saved Druckenmiller's 1999—and destroyed his 2000. "We thought it was the eighth inning, and it was the ninth," he reportedly told the *New York Times* a few months later, after the first leg of the crash, explaining "how the $8.2 billion Quantum Fund. . . wound up down 22 percent this year." Admirably forthright, Druckenmiller explained that

*Most people wouldn't be caught dead admitting they'd bought an "overvalued" stock, even though they'd been doing it successfully for years.

he had thought the rally would continue longer than it did.* "I screwed up," he concluded. "I overplayed my hand."

Druckenmiller took the fall and left the firm, and the press delighted in his "misguided investments" in "ridiculously priced" technology stocks. The real lessons, however, were similar to those of Long Term Capital Management, a massive hedge fund that had blown up two years earlier: 1) when investment performance is measured in weeks and months instead of decades, success and failure are arbitrary, and 2) even the smartest investors often get it wrong. In fact, even in hindsight, it was easier to condemn Robertson and Druckenmiller's mistakes than to identify what they were. Not straying from one's investment discipline? Straying from one's investment discipline? It was also easy to forget that neither Robertson nor Druckenmiller was working for himself. On the contrary, both men were employed in a profession in which impatient customers can—and quickly do—vote with their feet.

The press's autopsies of Robertson and Druckenmiller rarely mentioned the other (boring) truth: No style of investing works in all markets. Sometimes "growth" stocks take the lead. Sometimes "value" stocks do. Sometimes big stocks outperform small stocks. Sometimes "mid-caps" conquer all. In the end, most of these temporary trends average out: styles that outperform in one period under-perform in the next. The demand for dramatic, continual results, however, is such that assets will always flow toward styles that are working and away from those that aren't. The demand for dramatic stories about rising and falling stars, meanwhile, ensures that practitioners of whichever style is in vogue will be lionized and practitioners of whichever is not will be ridiculed.

At the end of the millennium, if you managed a fund and you didn't own technology stocks, you weren't "cautious" or "disciplined"—you were wrong. And for the eighteen months leading up to the spring of 2000, you couldn't afford to be wrong. No story illustrates this more clearly than that of another former client of mine, a man I'll call "The Pragmatist."

In early 2000, with the NASDAQ having doubled in a year, many professional investors were expecting a correction, but few were expecting a crash. The Pragmatist, however, *was* expecting a crash. In fact, he was expecting a crash severe enough to cripple his fund, and he had taken active steps to defend against this.

The Pragmatist had begun his career in the late 1980s, when technology stocks were out of favor, and he had stuffed his fund full of them, with marvelous results. Unlike managers who had bought technology stocks to mimic a benchmark or cash in on the sector *du jour*, The Pragmatist had owned them because his strategy was based on improving returns on capital. Early in the 1990s, after the personal computer industry bust, Microsoft, Intel and other surviving companies had had excellent returns on capital. Over the course of the decade, however, other investors had discovered the sector, and, as ever, when the supply of capital increases, returns drop.

In mid–1999, sticking to his discipline, The Pragmatist began dumping his technology holdings. Technology stocks kept going up, however, so, right away, his fund started to underperform. And right away, the complaints started rolling in. Irate fund holders would call during the day to get The Pragmatist's extension, and then call back at night to curse into his voice mail:

"You sack of shit—all my other funds are doing fine except this one. Just *buy technology*, you moron."

Like Jeff Vinik, The Pragmatist didn't lose money—his fund finished 1999 up about ten percent, a solid year in a normal decade. His performance didn't keep pace with the NASDAQ's, though (up 86%). As a result, the fund's inflows soon reversed, and money began gushing out the door. The complaints intensified, and, eventually, they came from above. The Pragmatist's boss, tired of hearing from infuriated shareholders—and tired of losing assets and the fees that came with them—began questioning his judgment, reminding him that almost everyone else believed that technology stocks would just keep going up.

By March 2000, The Pragmatist had whittled technology down from a third of his fund to about 10%. To put this in perspective, the S&P 500 was then composed of about 35% technology stocks, and many fund managers were at 50%. The less technology the Pragmatist owned, of course, the worse his relative performance got—and the more money flowed out of his fund. Finally, one day in early 2000, fed up with damage to the firm's reputation and bottom line, The Pragmatist's boss had had enough. This time, she didn't debate the merits of The Pragmatist's investment thesis. She just made it simple: Buy technology or you're fired.

"No matter how good your record is," The Pragmatist explained later, "you've only got ninety days."

The Pragmatist's first impulse was to quit. He soon realized, however, what would happen if he did: The firm would replace him with a fearless, twenty-four-year-old portfolio manager who would immediately go to a 50% tech weighting. The Pragmatist would forfeit his job and bonus, and, when the market imploded, his fund holders would get crushed anyway. If The Pragmatist refused to comply with his boss's order, meanwhile, he would get fired "for cause"—losing his bonus *and* severance and leaving the same empty chair to fill.

The Pragmatist, in other words, faced the ultimate investment risk vs. career risk dilemma. If he stood on principle—

either by quitting or getting fired—both he and his share-holders would lose big. The situation seemed hopeless, until he thought of a third option. What if he opted for a compromise solution, a practical solution, a solution that would make the outcome for his shareholders merely bad instead of catastrophic? What if he carried out his boss's order to "buy technology," but only went to a 25% weighting instead of the standard 35%–50%? Then he could keep his job and his bonus, and, when the market crashed, his shareholders would only lose half as much. And who knew? Maybe his boss was right. Maybe technology stocks *would* just keep going up.

The Pragmatist followed orders, went to 25% technology. Then, after the market crashed—and he got blamed—he quit the business.

The Greatest Danger of All

A Wall Street self-defense manual would not be complete if it did not address the greatest danger of all: you. Human beings, it turns out, are wired to make dumb investing mistakes. What's more, we are wired not to learn from them, but to make them again and again. The consolation? It's not our fault. We are born suckers.

In the past thirty years, academic research has progressed beyond efficient-markets theory, which mistook humans for robots, into behavioral finance, which acknowledges that we are, in fact, sweating, breathing, hoarding, pleasure-seeking, pain-avoiding herd animals who employ a looser definition of "rational" than computer chips. A full enumeration of the innate tendencies that doom most of us to investing mediocrity would be longer than this book. So, here are some highlights:

- *Self-attribution Bias*: We attribute our gains to ourselves, and we blame our losses on others or bad luck. This hobbles us in two ways. First, we don't learn from our mistakes because we don't see them as mistakes. Second, we assume we are skilled or smart when we're just lucky.
- *The Law of Small Numbers*: We make conclusions about market patterns, advisor skills and our own talent from

sample sizes that are too small to be meaningful. As a result, we conclude that markets and stocks are likely to go up or down when they aren't, that advisors are skilled or unskilled when they aren't, and that we are the second coming of Warren Buffett when we aren't.

- *Prospect Theory*: We have an irrational tendency to sell winners to lock in profits and keep losers to avoid taking losses. Among other errors, this causes us to prematurely generate capital-gains taxes (by selling winners) and miss the opportunity to harvest losses (by not selling losers).

- *Myopic Loss Aversion*: In certain circumstances, we refuse to make good bets that have a potentially painful outcome. This causes us to cling to bonds and cash even though they have performed worse than equities over the long haul.

- *Conservatism Bias* and *Confirmatory Bias*: Once we form opinions, we tend to overvalue information that reinforces them and undervalue information that undermines them (conservatism bias). We even tend to seek out supporting information (confirmatory bias). In other words, to paraphrase Simon and Garfunkel, we hear what we want to hear and disregard the rest.

- *Overoptimism*: We are overoptimistic and overconfident. According to strategist James Montier, when students are asked whether they will perform in the top half of their class, an average of 80% say yes. A similar percentage of drivers and investors believe they are above average. Innate overconfidence makes it easier for part-time hobbyists to dismiss a century's worth of academic research showing that the vast majority of even full-time professionals can't beat the market. *They* can't, we think. But *we* can.

- *Outcome Bias*: We evaluate decisions based on outcomes instead of probabilities. If a stock we buy goes up, we pat ourselves on the back, and, if it goes down, we chew ourselves (or our advisors) out. Thus, instead of focusing on *expected returns*, we congratulate ourselves for stupid choices that happen to turn out well and vow to never again make smart choices that happen to turn out badly. Our errors get reinforced, and our wise decisions rejected.

- *All That Glitters*: Professors Brad Barber and Terrance Odean discovered that we don't just buy *any* stocks, we buy stocks in the news. Why? Because we can't be bothered to sift through the thousands of stocks that aren't in the news, and because stocks in the news often have the investment attribute that we love most: Amazing past performance. Unfortunately, "past performance is not indicative of future returns," and we all watch the news—so any opportunity that might have existed is gone long before we click "buy."

- *The Testosterone Effect*: On average, Barber and Odean also discovered, men trade more than women. Consequently, men do worse than women. Way to go, boys.

- *Buffett's "Rearview Mirror" Bias*: We base our expectations for the future on what has happened in the recent past. Because markets are mean-reverting, this is dangerous: We are most bullish at the end of long bull markets, when we should be most bearish, and most bearish at the end of long bear markets, when we should be most bullish.

- *Hindsight Bias*: When we reflect on the past, we imagine that we knew what was going to happen when we actually didn't. As James Montier puts it, "You didn't know it all along, you just think you did." This allows us to imagine, for example, that we always knew that the tech boom of the late 1990s was a bubble and that everyone who suggested otherwise was an idiot or crook. It also makes us overconfident about our ability to predict what will happen next.

Want to Be a Better Investor? First, Get Brain Damage

We don't make investment mistakes because we're stupid, although our innate ability to assess probabilities is indeed weak. Mostly, we make mistakes because we're emotional. Even when we correctly assess probabilities, we're often unable or unwilling to act on them.

In 2005, a group of professors from Stanford, Carnegie Mellon and the University of Iowa conducted an experiment in which they gave subjects $20 apiece and invited them to participate in up to twenty rounds of "investment" decisions. The subjects consisted of two groups: 1) normal people, and 2) people with a specific type of brain damage—one that inhibited their ability to process emotions but had no effect on their IQs. In each round of the experiment, a coin was flipped. If the coin came up heads (50% chance), all participants lost $1.00. If the coin came up tails (50% chance), all participants won $2.50. The "expected return" for each round, therefore, was $1.25, more than the $1.00 placed at risk. This was a

Top Ten Rules of *Self* Self-Defense

- Remember that you are not as good an investor as you think you are
- Remember that you do not know what the market is going to do
- Remember that the best analysts in the world do not know what the market is going to do
- Remember that after bull markets you will want to buy, and after bear markets you will want to sell—and that this is the opposite of what you should do
- Remember that long-term investing means decades, not weeks
- Remember that the psychological tendencies that allowed your ancestors to survive on the savannah will help you screw yourself in the market
- Remember that "you didn't know it all along—you just think you did"
- Remember that brain-damaged people will out-trade you
- Remember that the fewer trades you make, the better
- Remember that the way to give yourself the best odds is to build a diversified portfolio of low-cost index funds and hold them forever

good bet, in other words, one that a "rational" investor would make every time.

As might be expected, both groups made money, but the brain-damaged folks made more. Why? Because they participated in more rounds (84% vs. 58%). Interestingly, the relative performance wasn't a matter of the brain-damaged people being smarter to begin with: Both groups started out by participating in the same percentage of rounds, but the normal people got more conservative as the experiment went on. The normal people, in other words, appeared to learn from previous rounds (irrationally, given that past coin flips have no bearing on future flips), and they learned the wrong lessons. Specifically, they learned that losing hurts. After participating in a round in which they lost $1.00, only 41% of normal subjects participated in the next round (vs. the 100% that should have).

The message? We're bad at making good bets that might cost us money, even when we have brain damage. And we get even worse at it after we feel the sting of loss.

Second, Get Humble and Stop Trading

Needless to say, 80% of drivers are not above average, and 80% of students do not perform in the top half of their classes. Similarly, most investors are not talented enough to beat the majority of other investors, even when they think they are. The difference between the innate overconfidence we have about our school abilities and our investing abilities is that 1) it is harder to tell whether we have beaten the market than whether we have finished in the top half of our class (thus making it easier for us to fool ourselves) and, 2) to beat the market, we do not just have to be "above average": We have to be *way* above average.

Professors Barber and Odean have conducted numerous studies that illustrate just how inept most of us are at the trading game, a flaw they attribute to overconfidence. For example, Barber and Odean studied 66,000 investors at a discount brokerage firm for the six years through 1997. They found that the performance of such investors paralleled that of mutual funds: Collectively, the investors performed slightly ahead of the market on a gross basis, but lagged it by 1% per year after transaction costs. Most of the investors traded small-cap stocks, moreover, and, compared to a more appropriate small-cap benchmark, the average lag was –4%. The performance of the most frequent traders lagged a whopping 7% below the benchmark.

As usual, the cause of the underperformance was overtrading: The investors would have done better if they had just bought and held. More distressingly, in this and other studies, *the stocks that the investors sold did better (after they sold them) than the stocks they bought.* So much for picking winners.

An even more depressing series of studies, conducted by a Boston-based firm called DALBAR, found that investors who trade mutual funds perform even worse than those who trade individual stocks. In the twenty years through 2004, a period in which the S&P 500 produced an annualized return of 12.98%, DALBAR found that the average equity mutual fund *investor* earned only 3.51%. The cause of this atrocious performance was not investors' selection of poor funds, but their inability to stick with *any* funds. The average investor held each fund for only two years. As with stocks, investors tended to pour money into funds after bull markets (rearview mirror bias, greed) and yank money out after bear markets (rearview mirror bias, fear), thus costing themselves money on both ends. Investors who tried to time the market—switching between stocks and cash—did even worse. These people *lost* an average of –3.29% per year.

DALBAR's most profound conclusion was that investors' bad trading habits cost them far more than choosing bad funds. Again, the greatest risk to your retirement nest egg is not the market or Wall Street. It's *you*.

Third, Ignore Others, Including the Crowd and (or Especially) Experts

Michael Mauboussin of Legg Mason, another leading expert on behavioral finance, has analyzed two of our most unsettling psychological tendencies: the extent to which we allow group-think to affect our decisions and our willingness to defer to authority. Both lead to expensive investing mistakes.

Mauboussin describes experiments conducted in the 1950s by psychologist Solomon Asch in which subjects were asked to make simple judgments in the presence of others. Unbeknownst to the one subject in each test, the other participants were actors. The group was asked easy questions—for example, "Which of these three lines is the same length as this other line?"—and then each person answered in turn. For the first few rounds, Asch's actors gave correct answers, and the subject got the question right almost every time. Then the actors started giving answers that were obviously wrong. Some of the subjects expressed shock at the group's mistakes, but a third of them simply went along with the crowd. As Mauboussin concludes, "group dynamics—often revealed as stock price performance—tempt investors to go along with the majority."

Mauboussin also describes the famous Milgram experiments, in which subjects who thought they were participating in an intelligence test were asked to administer a shock to another "subject" (an actor) each time the faux-subject got a question wrong. With each incorrect answer, the intensity of the shock increased. When subjects hesitated to administer

additional shocks—for example, when the actor was scream-
ing in agony or a gauge indicated that the shock's intensity had
reached a lethal level—the lab-coated test administrator simply said, "The experiment requires that you go on," or "It is
absolutely essential that you continue." The results were horri-
fying: Approximately half of the subjects administered shocks
that would have killed a real subject.

As Mauboussin concluded, "Investors—both professional
and individual—have a tendency to defer to perceived authority figures, including successful investors, strategies or other
market prognosticators." When I was an analyst, I saw both
sides of this. I placed too much stock in the opinions of those
who seemed to know more than I did (my fault, not theirs).
More unsettling, I saw others do the same with me.

News Flash: You're Human

People's natural tendency (here we go again . . .) is to view the
conclusions of behavioral finance theorists as more proof of
how dumb everyone else is rather than how handicapped we
all are as we try to outwit each other. But the biggest myth of
the 1990s—the biggest myth of every bull market—is that
picking winners is so easy that anyone can do it, that all you
have to do to win is play. The reality is that only a tiny handful
of people are dedicated and talented enough to overcome their
DNA, confront the long odds and come out ahead of the markets, and they are as rare as world-class athletes. As for the rest
of us, we may have fun trying (and this, in and of itself, may
be enough reason to play), but we are almost sure to lose.

PART 3
A SOLUTION

A Solution

At the beginning of this book, I promised to recommend an investment strategy that would allow you to have your cake and eat (a slice of) it, too. So here goes.

The strategy accepts that you are human and does not require that you act like a robot. It accepts that you may find speculating challenging, stimulating and fun, that you are innately (over)confident, and that you think you are one of the few investors talented enough to beat the market over the long haul. It accepts that you enjoy basking in the glow of your recent picks and making fun of friends who own index funds. It accepts that, however irrelevant market TV may be to intelligent investing, you like watching it, and you want to continue watching it, just as you want to continue speculating. It accepts that you may not care whether you "beat the market," that you may just want to have a good time. And it still allows you to generate an above average, after-tax, long-term return.

Here's the strategy:

First, divide your portfolio into two parts—an investment portion and a speculation/entertainment portion—and create a separate account for each. Even if you are not yet convinced that the odds on speculating are worse than the odds on investing, make the speculation portion small. (Ideally, make it less than 5% of your portfolio; any larger and you won't be guaranteed an above average long-term return).

Second, in the speculation account, do *whatever you want*. Pick stocks. Trade commodities. Hire and fire advisors. Short S&P futures. Buy deep out-of-the-money calls. Play the pink sheets. Time the market. Chase performance. Read charts. Buy independent research (with money from the speculation account). Scan chat boards. Trade 24-7. In other words, try as hard as you can to beat the market. Do this for a decade, learning from your mistakes and paying all your speculation costs and taxes out of the speculation account. Then, taking care to calculate your performance correctly, compare it to that of your investment account. If you have soundly beaten the investment portfolio, note that your overall performance (the sum of both accounts) will have beaten the market—and celebrate: You will now have a better ten-year record than the majority of investors, including professionals. If you're confident you can keep this performance up, continue speculating for another decade. If you're still ahead after twenty years, and still enjoying yourself, then hats off to you. You won't know for certain that you have skill, but you will certainly have the experience necessary to make that determination yourself.

Meanwhile. . .

Establish your *investment* account, which should contain at least 95% of your current and future savings, at a high-quality firm offering a wide selection of *low-cost* advisory services, brokerage services, and funds. (Vanguard and TIAA-CREF are excellent choices; Fidelity, Charles Schwab and other firms offer *some* low-cost products, but they also offer high-cost ones, so be selective.) Sign up for a basic portfolio evaluation, which will consist of questions about your assets, risk tolerance, goals, time horizon, etc., and a brief phone consultation with an advisor. This will produce a recommended investment plan, which should contain target allocations to stocks, bonds, real estate and cash. The precise allocations aren't crucial—it's the diversification and cost control that matter—but if you want a sanity check, get similar recommendations from other firms. Then implement the plan, using low-cost index funds and ETFs as the primary tools.

Be sure to have all dividends and capital gains distributions reinvested. Set up a direct deposit system that automatically zaps a meaningful chunk of every paycheck into the account, and invest the new cash in the fund that has recently done the *worst*. This will help re-balance the portfolio and ensure that you get the highest expected return for every new investment dollar. Check the account occasionally to make sure that the money is still there. If necessary, after more than a year, re-balance to ensure that the risk/return profile remains acceptable. (Try to avoid selling funds in which you have embedded capital gains, though—you'll rack up tax and transaction costs.) After five years, get another evaluation to see whether the same asset allocation strategy makes sense. After another five years, get another. And so on.

Alternatively, just buy a low-cost life cycle fund, and let the fund firm worry about new allocations and re-balancing. Most life cycle funds contain a reasonable mix of domestic and international stocks, bonds and cash, one that changes as you age and your investment time horizon becomes shorter. Life cycle funds are not perfect. Age is only one factor in determining appropriate asset allocation, and life cycle funds are not tailored to the specific circumstances of each investor. Many life cycle funds also do not yet include REITs or TIPS, but the fund firms will probably address this shortcoming eventually. The reason life cycle funds are still a good choice is that they provide the long-term discipline and patience that most investors lack. And you can always supplement a life cycle fund with a real-estate index fund and whatever other funds are necessary to achieve the desired allocation mix.

If you want a dedicated financial advisor, find one whose fees are less than 1% of assets per year, who understands the importance of asset allocation and cost control, and/or uses a firm called Dimensional Fund Advisors. Dimensional offers a range of relatively low-cost passive funds designed to take advantage of the "small" and "value" effects I described earlier. Dimensional does not sell funds directly to individuals—you have to use a specially trained independent advisor—but you will get something unique for your money. Regardless of which firm your advisor uses, make sure that he or she focuses on generating the highest possible *net, after-tax, risk-adjusted* return. Taxes, fees and transaction costs are the only elements of your return that the advisor can control, so make sure that he or she concentrates on them.

A final word of caution: I have not devoted much of this book to forecasting long-term asset returns, but I believe it is possible to get a reasonable sense of what they might be. And the bad news is that—for the next decade or two—they are likely to be worse than they have been over the last couple of decades. Why? Because the valuations of all major asset classes (with the exception of cash) are still high. From time immemorial, a couple of decades of above-average performance (and the resulting high valuations) have heralded a couple of decades of below-average performance. In all likelihood, therefore, for both stocks and bonds, we are in the early years

---

Top Ten Rules of Intelligent Investing

- Reduce costs
- Draw a distinction between investing and entertainment
- Diversify among major, mean-reverting asset classes
- Focus on after-cost, after-tax, after-inflation, risk-adjusted returns
- Manage your expectations
- Don't transact unless you absolutely have to
- Don't try to beat the market
- Don't get distracted by short-term noise (and remember that it's most of what you hear)
- Don't hire full-service advisors unless you are confident they will add more value than a low-cost, passive life cycle fund
- Remember that the greatest risk to your return is you

---

of a secular bear market, one that will result in mediocre returns for at least another decade.

This is depressing, but there is little you can do about it, and your attempts to try (stock-picking, market timing, etc.) will likely just compound the problem. Eventually, valuations and performance should revert to or beyond long-term means, and, when they do, the table will be set for another big bull market. The longer the bear market in stocks and bonds lasts, of course, the more you will itch to dump them and invest in commodities, hedge funds, art, land or other hot products *du jour*. Try to resist this temptation. If it makes you feel better, allocate a small portion of your portfolio to a low-cost commodity fund or a fund of funds and keep a larger-than-usual percentage in cash. But don't forget that, over the long run, equities should provide the best inflation-adjusted return, and that, the more stock prices sag, the better off you will be (because you will be able to buy more shares cheaply with your monthly savings). This—along with your other Wall Street self-defense techniques—will put you in an ideal position for the eventual return of the bull.

Afterword

Thus ends your short course in Wall Street self-defense. I hope it helps. I hope it helps you manage—and meet—your long-term expectations. I hope it helps you resist the charms of some would-be advisors, as well as understand how much their help will really cost. I hope it persuades you that stock picking, market timing and fund picking not only consume time and create stress but usually reduce returns. I hope it explains why passive investing does not "guarantee mediocrity" but, instead, leaves most other strategies in the dust.

I hope this book does all that, but I don't expect it to. Why not? Because, in the investing realm, you should never take any one opinion as gospel. In my experience, it takes time to embrace these concepts, to be confident that costs really *do* matter, that most pros really *don't* beat passive benchmarks, that you probably *can't* time the market, that picking winners *is* harder than it sounds. These concepts run so counter to common wisdom and common sense that it will likely take you a while to accept them. I merely hope, therefore, that this book will help nudge you along.

To make the process easier—and to give you some ammo to use against those who dismiss these ideas with a thousand variants of "Well, that's just ridiculous. Of course you can beat the market! I've beaten the market the last three years!" —I have provided a *Further Reading* list. It includes some of the books, articles, studies and web sites that helped persuade me that, for most people, low-cost passive investing is the intelligent way to go. I have also posted the list online, at www.wallstreetselfdefense.com.

In short, I hope that this book helps you earn a better long-term return. I wish it could tell you how to "Get Rich in the Market!!!," but, unfortunately, the surest way to do that is to save more. In fact, as you continue your education in Wall Street self-defense, always remember this: Every percentage point of after-tax, after-cost, *real* return you earn will indeed make a big difference to your future nest egg. No matter how much time and money you invest in learning how to invest, however, the most important contributors to your wealth will never change: The age at which you start investing, and the amount you add along the way.

A Final Note

A decade ago, in the late 1990s, I had the privilege of having millions of people around the world often listen to what I had to say. I didn't take this privilege for granted, and I didn't let the attention go to my head. I took the responsibility that came with it very seriously. That said, it wasn't until after the era had passed—or, rather, had been blasted out of existence—that I understood just what an intense privilege and responsibility it had been.

Even before the regulatory disaster, one regret I had from my analyst years was the feeling that, by missing the top of the Internet bubble, I had let people down. I had made several good calls on the way up, and I was hoping that, if that amazing boom was, in fact, about to end, I would spot the change in time to make another one. With the benefit of more experience, I see that my real mistake was thinking that I might be able to precisely call the top, but whatever the error, the regret is the same.

In life, you don't get do-overs, and you never stop getting chances to learn from mistakes. In the better-late-than-never department, though, I have one final hope for this book. I hope that, this time, even in hindsight, both you and I will be able to look back and think, "Now, *that* was good advice."

Further Reading

The following list is designed to help readers explore concepts discussed in this book in more detail. A more extensive and updated list may be found online at www.wallstreetselfdefense.com.

Books

Stocks for the Long Run, by Jeremy Siegel
Irrational Exuberance, by Robert Shiller
Winning the Loser's Game, by Charles Ellis
Common Sense on Mutual Funds, by John Bogle
A Random Walk Down Wall Street, by Burton Malkiel
Unconventional Success, by David Swensen
Investment Management, by Robert Hagin
The Intelligent Investor (Revised Edition), by Benjamin Graham
Index Funds, by Mark Hebner
Against the Gods: The Remarkable Story of Risk, by Peter Bernstein

Free Web-Based Analysis and Commentary

Economic analysis: Paul Kasriel and Asha Bangalore of Northern Trust
Asset-class forecasts: Monthly asset-class forecasts from Grantham, Mayo, van Otterloo

Market commentary: Jeremy Grantham's quarterly letters at www.gmo.com; Andrew Smithers, Smithers & Co. (occasional free articles); William Gross's monthly letters, www.pimco.com.

Personal investing: Jonathan Clements, *Wall Street Journal*; Jason Zweig, *Money*; John Bogle, speeches and editorials.

Investment wisdom: Warren Buffett's annual letters; Michael Mauboussin, Mauboussin on Strategy, Legg Mason.

Notes

Part I: A Self-Defense Framework

Chapter 1: How to Get Rich

The "How to Get Rich" calculation assumes a 9.8% annual net return for 50 years. According to Ibbotson Associates, since 1926, large U.S. stocks have returned 10.4% per year. I assume a similar gross return over the next 50 years, minus a modest fee for a low-cost index fund. As noted, the calculation does not account for taxes or inflation and assumes the reinvestment of all dividends.

The "How to Get Taken to the Cleaners" calculation assumes a 10% gross return for 50 years, less fund expenses of 1.5% per year. The expenses are deducted at the end of each year, based on the year-end account value. If the expenses had been deducted at the end of each quarter or based on the *average* account value, the result would be slightly different. Why subtract the expenses? Because the net return of the average mutual fund lags the appropriate passive benchmark by approximately the amount of the fund's costs (see, for example, Wermers, 2000, or Carhart, 1997). According to the Investment Company Institute, the average expense ratio for an equity mutual fund in 2005 was 1.54%. In my example, reducing the fund's market lag to 1% per year would result in a 50-year balance of about $7 million instead of $6 million (i.e., it would still cost you

$4 million). Increasing the lag to 2% would result in an ending balance of about $4 million (and cost you $7 million).

The $1 million in fees is the approximate amount that a fund owner would pay to the fund manager over 50 years if the fund charged 1.5% per year and earned a 10% gross return. The $5 million in lost compounding is the approximate amount the fees would have generated had they remained in the fund owner's account.

The observation that frequent trading will probably cost you money is based on research by University of California professors Brad Barber and Terrance Odean. The inflation estimate assumes 3% inflation, in line with the 3.1% historical average reported by Ibbotson Associates.

Chapter 3: Why Bother?

The "safe withdrawal rate" of 4% is based on a study by Philip L. Cooley, Carl M. Hubbard and Daniel T. Walz, finance professors at Trinity University in San Antonio, Texas (published in the *AAII Journal* in February, 1998). The professors studied actual market returns from 1926 to 1995 and, from them, evaluated a range of portfolios, withdrawal periods and withdrawal rates. The professors concluded that a portfolio of 75% stocks and 25% bonds in which withdrawals were adjusted for inflation had a 98% chance of lasting 30 years at a withdrawal rate of 4% per year, an 83% chance at 5% per year, a 68% chance at 6% a year and so on. The study did not account for taxes, transaction costs or advisory fees: Investors who pay these costs would have a significantly lower safe withdrawal rate.

The appropriate withdrawal rate for any particular individual depends on the individual's risk tolerance, other sources of income, the desired trade-off between current spending and future safety, the expected length of the payout period, and other factors. For shorter payout periods, higher withdrawal rates would be sustainable.

The inflation-impact estimates are mine. I subtracted 3% of the value in the first year, 3% of the remainder in the second year, and so on. I assumed the "forty-year-old who stuffs his cash under a mattress" would retire in 25 years, at age 65.

Chapter 4: A Short History of Market History

The data in "Long Term Total Returns, 1925–2005" comes from Ibbotson Associates' *Stocks, Bonds, Bills, and Inflation 2006 Yearbook*. Similar returns are reported by Wharton professor Jeremy Siegel in *Stocks For The Long Run* and many other researchers.

The U.S. stock market price data in the 20th century summary is from Yale professor Robert Shiller, the author of *Irrational Exuberance*. The time required for investors to recoup their losses after 1929 including the value of dividends is from Jeremy Siegel's *The Future for Investors*.

The article by Warren Buffett, "Warren Buffett on the Stock Market," appeared in the December 10, 2001, issue of *Fortune*. This article and a similar one by Buffett in 1999 are worth the cost of an online subscription.

The theory that the equity risk premium may shrink in the future is discussed by many experts, including Elroy Dimson, Paul Marsh and Mike Staunton in *Triumph of the Optimists* and Ibbotson Associates. Economist Andrew Smithers, Yale's Robert Shiller, money manager Jeremy Grantham, and others argue that, irrespective of the risk premium, equity returns in the next decade or two will be below average because, measured correctly (with a cyclically adjusted P-E ratio), the U.S. stock market is still expensive. The market's historical cyclicality—a decade up, a decade or two flat, etc.—supports this view.

The "dissection" of equity returns is based on data from Ibbotson Associates, Buffett's *Fortune* articles, Ed Easterling's *Unexpected Returns: Understanding Secular Stock Market Cycles* and other sources.

Chapter 5: How Rich You Can Get

The future wealth calculations are based on straight-line appreciation at the stated rates each year. The cost estimates are derived from numerous sources, including John Bogle's *Common Sense on Mutual Funds,* the Investment Company Institute's 2006 *Fact Book,* Ibbotson Associates' estimate of long-term inflation data and ballpark federal and state tax rates. The resulting net, after-tax, real returns are back-of-the-envelope estimates and are not intended to represent precise calculations of compound returns. Exact costs and tax rates will vary for each investor, as will returns. Furthermore, if I had subtracted 8% costs each year from a 10% gross return, instead of projecting a 2% net return each year, the final values would have been lower.

Chapter 6: So, Just Beat the Market!

As noted, definitions of "active" and "passive" vary, as do those of "beating the market." The logic that the return on the average actively managed dollar must lag that of the average passive benchmark comes from Professor William Sharpe's *The Arithmetic of Active Management.* The concept is discussed in Charles Ellis's *Winning the Loser's Game,* Mark Hebner's *Index Funds: The 12-Step Program for Active Investors,* and other sources. A detailed example (mine) follows:

Assume a market comprises four stocks—A, B, C and D—each of which have one share. Assume A and B go up 30% and 15%, respectively, and C and D go down 5% and 10%, respectively. On an equal-weighted basis, the market return will be 7.5%.

The Market

Stock	Return
A	30%
B	15%
C	–5%
D	–10%
	7.5%

Assume further that two active investors trade the market, and, between them, own the market (i.e., they are the only investors trading the market). If each investor owns two stocks, there are six performance scenarios for the period, as illustrated in the table below. Note that, in all scenarios, the average performance of the two investors *equals* that of the market. Note further that in no scenario do *both* investors beat the market. Lastly, note that, when one investor beats the market, the other lags it.

Scenarios	Portfolios		Performance		Aggregate	
	Mgr 1	Mgr 2	Mgr 1	Mgr 2	Avg Mgr 1+ 2	Market
1	A,B	C,D	22.5%	−7.5%	7.5%	7.5%
2	A,C	B,D	12.5%	2.5%	7.5%	7.5%
3	A,D	B,C	10.0%	5.0%	7.5%	7.5%
4	B,C	A,D	5.0%	10.0%	7.5%	7.5%
5	B,D	A,C	2.5%	12.5%	7.5%	7.5%
6	C,D	A,B	−7.5%	22.5%	7.5%	7.5%

Now, assume that each investor is a mutual fund manager who charges a 1% active management fee. In each case, this fee is subtracted from the manager's gross performance to yield his or her net return. Note that, now, the aggregate return of both managers *lags the market in every scenario.*

Same Scenarios With 1% Active Management Fee

Scenarios	Gross Performance		Net Return		Average Net Return	
	Mgr 1	Mgr 2	Mgr 1	Mgr 2	Avg Mgr 1+ 2	Market
1	22.5%	−7.5%	21.5%	−8.5%	6.5%	7.5%
2	12.5%	2.5%	11.5%	1.5%	6.5%	7.5%
3	10.0%	5.0%	9.0%	4.0%	6.5%	7.5%
4	5.0%	10.0%	4.0%	9.0%	6.5%	7.5%
5	2.5%	12.5%	1.5%	11.5%	6.5%	7.5%
6	−7.5%	22.5%	−8.5%	21.5%	6.5%	7.5%

Lastly, assume that a third manager pursues a passive strategy in which he holds all four stocks (in this case, assume each stock has two shares). Assume that, because the passive manager does not have research costs, he charges only a 0.25% management fee (typical). Note that the passive manager beats at least one of the active managers in *every scenario*.

Same Scenarios With 1% Active Management Fee and a Passive Manager With a 0.25% Fee

Scenarios	Gross Performance			Net Return			Aggregate		
	Mgr 1	Mgr 2	Passive	Mgr 1	Mgr 2	Passive	Avg 1+2	Passive	Market
1	22.5%	–7.5%	7.5%	21.5%	–8.5%	7.25%	6.5%	7.25%	7.5%
2	12.5%	2.5%	7.5%	11.5%	1.5%	7.25%	6.5%	7.25%	7.5%
3	10.0%	5.0%	7.5%	9.0%	4.0%	7.25%	6.5%	7.25%	7.5%
4	5.0%	10.0%	7.5%	4.0%	9.0%	7.25%	6.5%	7.25%	7.5%
5	2.5%	12.5%	7.5%	1.5%	11.5%	7.25%	6.5%	7.25%	7.5%
6	–7.5%	22.5%	7.5%	–8.5%	21.5%	7.25%	6.5%	7.25%	7.5%

Is the real world more complicated? Yes. But the same concepts apply. The biggest difference between this example and the real world is that most investors own a mix of "markets." Most stock investors, for example, keep some money in cash. In a period in which the stock market is rising rapidly, the return on stocks dwarfs the returns on cash, so the cash acts as a drag on the return. Similarly, in down markets, the cash reduces the overall loss. An investor with a significant cash position, therefore, may beat the stock market in bear markets and lag it in bull markets, but not because of superior stock-picking skill. If a trader is skilled at market timing—moving money into and out of the market at the right times—then the performance would be the result of skill. Few traders can do this consistently, however.

The assertion that between 33% and 97% of mutual funds lag the market comes from a review of many studies that have analyzed this question. The most basic studies compare the performance of all equity mutual funds with that of the Vanguard S&P 500 fund. The most favorable of such studies (from a stock picker's perspective) conclude that, on a pretax basis, about a third of funds beat the S&P 500 fund. (Princeton professor Burton Malkiel cites this percentage in a *Random Walk Down Wall Street*.)

More rigorous studies account for "survivorship bias"—the tendency for poor performing funds to cease operations and, thereby, drop out of the databases. They also compare funds with benchmarks that have similar style and size characteristics (small cap vs. small cap, for example). One study that adjusted for survivorship bias but not for style and size characteristics, *How Well Have Taxable Investors Been Served in the 1980s and 1990s,* by Robert D. Arnott, Andrew L. Berkin, and Jia Ye of First Quadrant, L.P., found that, depending on the time period, between 5% and 22% of funds beat the Vanguard S&P 500 on a pretax basis. On an after-tax basis, the percentage ranged from 5% to 16%.

A 1999 study by John Bogle, described in a speech entitled *Equity Fund Selection: The Needle or the Haystack,* found that over the prior thirty years, 186 of 355 funds—more than half—had ceased to exist. Of the surviving 169 funds, 113 lagged the market by more than 1% per year, 47 posted returns within 1% of the market (plus or minus), and 9 beat the market by more than 1% per year. According to this study, only 2.5% of the original 355 funds beat the market by more than 1% per year. Before the fact, therefore, your odds of randomly picking a winner would have been 1-in-40.

Chapter 7: Meet Your Competition

The list of research resources enjoyed by the average professional investor is mine. Charles Ellis is even more persuasive in *Winning the Loser's Game*. As an aside, it is eternally baffling to investment professionals that people outside the industry speak of a "level playing field" in which the average part-time, CNBC-watching doctor or dentist can expect to go head to head with the average hedge fund. The field is not level—the average professional processes more information in a day than the average amateur does in a year—but this is beside the point. In most pursuits, people would consider it absurd if part-time amateurs expected to compete with full-time professionals. In investing, however, people find the idea perfectly reasonable. The truth: It is as silly to think that a cardiologist could browse *Barrons* and compete against Fidelity as it would be to think that a portfolio manager could glance at a medical magazine and do heart surgery. Ignore all talk of a "level playing field." It is both illusory and misleading.

Chapter 8: The Vast and Unappreciated Role of Luck

The coin-prediction contest example is mine, but others have used similar examples, including Fred Schwed, Jr. in *Where Are the Customers' Yachts?* and Warren Buffett in "The Superstars of Graham-and-Doddsville," an article published in 1984 and reproduced in a recent edition of Benjamin Graham's *The Intelligent Investor*. Nassim Nicholas Taleb's *Fooled By Randomness: The Hidden Role of Chance in Life and in the Markets* describes how the tendency to mistake luck for skill pervades most human experience.

The superior performance of small stocks and value stocks is discussed extensively in the academic literature. Rolf W. Banz was the first to explore the size premium, in a 1981 paper entitled "The Relationship Between Returns and Market Value of Common Stocks," published in the *Journal of Financial Economics*. In the early 1990s, University of Chicago professor Eugene Fama and Dartmouth professor Kenneth French developed the "three-factor" model, which shows that stock returns can be explained (and predicted) by ranking stocks on value and size factors. Many other researchers have since explored the size and value effects, including Mark Carhart, Dimson et al in *Triumph of the Optimists,* Ibbotson Associates and others.

The data on the Beardstown Ladies is drawn from news stories.

Chapter 9: The Trouble with "Cheap" and "Expensive"

The intrinsic-value calculations in the "$1 a year forever" example are mine. The S&P data come from professor Shiller, who cyclically adjusts the P-E ratios by taking an average of 10-years' worth of earnings. As described, this adjustment minimizes the impact of the business cycle on corporate profit margins, a factor that significantly affects current-year P-E ratios. My "average P-E" is an arithmetic average of Shiller's annual P-Es from 1881–2000.

The "deathbed quote" from Benjamin Graham was published in a *Journal of Finance* interview in 1976. Several writers have subsequently cited it, including Robert Hagin in *Investment Management: Portfolio Diversification, Risk, and Timing—Fact and Fiction,* who was kind enough to steer me to the original source.

Chapter 10: Serenity Prayer for the Intelligent Investor

David Swensen's asset class recommendations are drawn from his excellent book *Unconventional Success, A Fundamental Approach to Personal Investment.* The data on Index Funds Advisors' portfolios comes from Mark Hebner's book *Index Funds.* This information is also available on IFA's web site: www.ifa.com.

Chapter 11: The Only Part of Your Return You Can Control

Any discussion of the impact of investment costs on returns owes a debt to John Bogle, the founder of Vanguard. Bogle is fond of saying that, with investment products, "you get what you don't pay for." Bogle's *Common Sense on Mutual Funds* was one source for the transaction-cost estimates. Others include Robert Hagin's *Investment Management* and Brad Barber and Terrance Odean's "Trading is Hazardous to Your Wealth."

Other researchers who have demonstrated the negative impact of costs include Russ Wermers, Mark Carhart, Charles Ellis, Burton Malkiel and the Securities and Exchange Commission. The return and tax-impact estimates are mine.

Chapter 12: A Self-Defense Preparedness Quiz

David Swensen's long-term return comes from *Unconventional Success*. Warren Buffett's long-term return comes from the 2005 Berkshire Hathaway letter to shareholders. It is worth noting that Buffett's return is not a public stock portfolio return but the annual compounded increase in book value for Berkshire Hathaway. It is also worth noting that the majority of the return (in percentage terms) came when Berkshire Hathaway was a much smaller company. Buffett himself has often observed that Berkshire's current vastness will dampen future returns.

Part II: Practicing Self-Defense

Chapter 13: Investment Advisors

The impact-of-fees calculations in "To Hire or Not to Hire" are mine. I deducted the fees each year at the end of the year, based on the year-end balance. The resulting account balances are compared to that of an account with the same gross return, 10%, and no fees. The information on the Vanguard Target Retirement 2035 Fund is taken from Vanguard's web site.

The price information for the DOW from 1966–2000 in "Beware Projected Returns" is from Yahoo! Finance. The bond return data for 1966–1982 is from Siegel's *Stocks for the Long Run*. The data on the ten-year trailing S&P 500 return during the 1970s and 1980s is from Ibbotson Associates' *SBBI Yearbook*.

The fee-, cost-, and inflation-impact calculations in "Beware Costs" are mine. As in Chapter 5, the "Back of the Envelope Real Return" is only a rough estimate. The precise impact would depend on the timing of the fee deductions, as well as the performance of the various asset classes (which have different fees associated with them). If the return had been calculated by subtracting the total costs each year, their true impact would have been slightly greater (i.e., the real return would be slightly lower).

In a 1997 study published in *The Journal of Finance,* "On Persistence in Mutual Fund Performance," Mark M. Carhart found that market, style, momentum and expense factors, not manager skill, explain almost all of the persistence of returns.

Chapter 14: Mutual Funds

The number of mutual funds is from the 2006 Investment Company Fact Book.

"Strategy One" to increase the odds of picking above-average funds is mine. It is based on studies showing that 1) the most expensive funds usually perform the worst, 2) the poor performance of the worst-performing funds persists, and 3) smaller active funds often perform better than large active funds. I also assumed that a for-profit firm has more incentive to charge fat fees and emphasize near-term performance than a nonprofit firm. (David Swensen makes the same observation in *Unconventional Success.*) I have not back-tested this strategy, and, as the final instruction—"Throw darts"—should suggest, it is decidedly unscientific. Strategy One is almost certainly inferior to "Strategy Two"—pick low-cost index funds. As far as I know, there is no strategy for picking future top-performing funds other than Two that has been shown to work consistently.

The Russ Wermers' study cited in "Money for Nothing" was published in the *Journal of Finance* in August 2000. It is entitled "Mutual Fund Performance: An Empirical Decomposition into Stock-Picking Talent, Style, Transactions Costs, and Expenses."

The First Quadrant study cited in "Active Funds Are Simply a Bad Bet" was conducted by Robert D. Arnott, Andrew L. Berkin and Jia

Ye from First Quadrant, L.P., in 2000. The study is entitled "The Management and Mismanagement of Taxable Assets."

For those still tempted to try to pick mutual fund winners, the conclusion from Mark Carhart's exhaustive 1997 study summarizes the current thinking of most rigorous mutual fund researchers:

> While the popular press will no doubt continue to glamorize the best-performing mutual fund managers, the mundane explanations of strategy and investment costs account for almost all of the important predictability in mutual fund returns.

In "A Fund-Picking Exercise," the data on the three funds came from the funds' 2006 prospectuses. The after-tax performance figures are after capital gains, dividends, and the sale of fund shares, as reported in each prospectus. These figures do not include state and local taxes.

The comparisons of the hypothetical cost impact on future relative performance are mine. I assume the same gross performance for both funds: 10% per year for 50 years. Loads and expense ratios are based on an initial investment of $100,000. The expenses are deducted at the end of each year, based on the year-end balance.

The data on S&P 500 index fund costs and performance comes from "Are Investors Rational? Choices among Index Funds" by Edwin J. Elton, Martin J. Gruber and Jeffrey A. Busse, published in *The Journal of Finance,* January, 2004. The study about investors' failure to understand the impact of fees is entitled "Why Does the Law of One Price Fail? An Experiment on Index Mutual Funds," by James J. Choi, David Laibson and Brigitte C. Madrian, May, 2006.

Rob Arnott's conclusions about fundamental indexing are drawn from *Fundamental Indexation*, by Robert D. Arnott, Jason Hsu, and Philip Moore, published in *The Financial Analysts Journal, 2005.* Wharton's Jeremy Siegel has written several articles about the subject, as has John Bogle. Dimensional Fund Advisors has published papers describing its fundamental indexing methodology.

The Little Book That Beats the Market, by Joel Greenblatt, was published by Wiley in 2005.

Chapter 15: Hedge Funds and Funds of Funds

The data on hedge funds are drawn from *Hedge Funds: Performance, Risk, and Capital Formation,* by William Fung, David A. Hsieh, Narayan Y. Naik and Tarun Ramadori, version dated March 10, 2006. *Hedge Funds: An Industry in Its Adolescence,* by William Fung and David A. Hsieh, Federal Reserve Bank of Atlanta, Financial Market Conference 2006, draft dated June 20, 2006. *Hedge Fung Benchmarks: Information Content and Biases,* by William Fung and David A. Hsieh; and *Hedge Funds: Risk and Return,* by Burton G. Malkiel and Atanu Saha.

The calculations of the impact of fees on gross returns are mine. For all funds, I deducted fees at the end of each year, based on the year-end balance (and, in the case of the hedge fund and fund of funds, the gain for the year). The S&P 500 fund calculation assumes an asset-based fee of 0.20% per year. The hedge fund calculation assumes an asset-based fee of 2% per year and a success fee of 20% of gains. The fund-of-funds calculation assumes a total asset-based fee of 3% per year (2% for the underlying hedge funds and an additional 1% for the fund of funds) and a success fee of 28% of the gross gain (10% of the fund-of-funds' net gain after paying fees of 20% of the gross gain to underlying hedge funds).

To calculate the relative impact of taxes, I assumed that the S&P 500 fund generated a net, pretax return of 10%. I further assumed that 100% of the return came from dividends and realized long-term gains, which I taxed at 20%. The latter assumptions overstate the tax drag on most S&P 500 funds, which have low realized gains. If, instead, I had assumed that the fund had generated most of its return from unrealized gains, the annual taxes would have been lower but the taxes on the "sale of fund shares" would have been higher.

For the hedge fund and fund of funds, I assumed that 75% of the return came from realized short-term gains, which I taxed at 50%, and that the remainder came from dividends and realized long-term gains, which I taxed at 20%. Funds that generate more return from unrealized gains, realized long-term gains, or dividends, or offset more of the short-term gains with realized short-term losses, create a lower tax liability. On the other hand, hyperactive, tax-blind funds generate an even larger tax liability.

The calculations of the relative impact of fees and taxes use the same assumptions as above. To be clear: The exact fee and tax load of each fund is different. The point of this exercise is merely to illustrate that all gains are not created equal and that hedge funds and funds of funds can crush the after-tax returns of taxable investors.

Hedge fund risk information was drawn from *10 Things Investors Should Know about Hedge Funds* by Harry M. Kat, Alternative Investment Research Centre, Cass Business School, City University, London, version dated January 6, 2003. Also helpful was *Hedge Funds: Risk and Return* by Burton G. Malkiel and Atanu Saha, which articulated similar conclusions.

The concept of passive "factors" that explain most hedge fund returns (similar to the Fama-French "three-factor model" and Carhart "four-factor model" that explain most equity returns) is drawn from several papers, including *Hedge Fund Benchmarks: A Risk Based Approach,* by William Fung and David A. Hsieh, March, 2004; *Making Sense of Hedge Fund Returns: What Matters and What Doesn't,* by George Martin, Research Director, Center for International Securities and Derivatives Markets, University of Massachusetts; *Asset-Based Style Factors for Hedge Funds,* by William Fung and David A. Hsieh; and *Hedge Fund Returns: You Can Make Them Yourself!,* by Harry M. Kat and Helder P. Palaro, version dated June 8, 2005.

Chapter 18: A Cautionary Tale of Market Wizards

The stories in this chapter are drawn from contemporaneous news sources, including the *Wall Street Journal* and the *New York Times*, as well as interviews I conducted from 2002–2005. The experiences of Jeff Vinik (Fidelity), Julian Robertson (Tiger) and Stan Druckenmiller

(Soros) were covered extensively by the financial press. The Pragmatist's experiences were not.

I related similar versions of these stories in "On Google, Bubbles, and Market Madness," *Fortune,* June 27, 2005.

Chapter 19: The Greatest Danger of All

Most of the tendencies mentioned in this chapter are described in the academic literature. For example, "Prospect Theory" was developed by psychologists Daniel Kahnemann and Amos Tversky and introduced in a 1979 paper in *Econometrica* called "Prospect Theory: An Analysis of Decision Under Risk." "Self-attribution bias" has been discussed by Hersh Shefrin, *Beyond Greed and Fear: Understanding Behavioral Finance and the Pyschology of Investing,* James Montier, *Darwin's Mind: The Evolutionary Foundations of Heuristics and Biases,* and others. Sources for the "Law of Small Numbers" include *Inferences by Believers in the Law of Small Numbers,* by Matthew Rabin, University of California, Berkeley, January 27, 2000. For additional discussion of these topics, as well as "myopic loss aversion," "overoptimism," "conservatism bias," and "confirmation bias," see www.behavioural finance.net.

The tendency I label "outcome bias" has been described by, among others, former Secretary of the Treasury Robert Rubin. The tendency I call "the testosterone effect" is described by University of California professors Brad Barber and Terrance Odean in *Boys Will Be Boys: Gender, Overconfidence, and Common Stock Investment,* February, 2001. "All That Glitters" comes from another Barber and Odean paper: *All That Glitters: The Effect of Attention and News on the Buying Behavior of Individual and Institutional Investors,* January, 2005. The tendency to develop future expectations by looking at the recent past ("rearview mirror bias") is described by Warren Buffett in the aforementioned *Fortune* articles. James Montier, a strategist at Dresdner Kleinwort Wasserstein, writes extensively about behavioral finance: See, for example, the *Seven Sins of Fund Management: A Behavioural Critique.*

The "brain damage" experiment is drawn from "Investment Behavior and the Negative Side of Emotion" by Baba Shiv, George Lowenstein, Antoine Bechara, Hanna Damasio and Antonio Damasio, *Pyschological Science,* 2005.

Brad Barber, Terrance Odean and others have studied investors' propensity to be overconfident and over-trade. Notable papers include, "Volume, Volatility, Price, and Profit: When All Traders Are Above Average" (Odean, *The Journal of Finance,* December 1998), "Do Investors Trade Too Much?" (Odean, *The American Economic Review,* December 1999), and "Learning to be Overconfident" (Odean and Simon Gervais, *The Review of Financial Studies,* Spring 2001). The specific study referenced here is "Trading Is Hazardous to Your Wealth: The Common Stock Investment Performance of Individual Investors," Barber and Odean, *The Journal of Finance,* April 2000.

The DALBAR conclusions are from DALBAR's Quantitative Analysis of Investor Behavior, 2006. DALBAR conducts this study annually, but does not reveal its precise methodology, so the conclusions cannot be evaluated. In *Investment Management,* Robert Hagin cites research by Laurence Siegel that concludes that average fund investors earn higher returns than DALBAR calculates, but still far less than if they had bought and held.

Michael J. Mauboussin, the chief investment strategist at Legg Mason, first discussed the Asch and Milgram experiments in the *Consilient Observer* series he wrote at Credit Suisse First Boston. An updated version of the analysis, *Getting Out of Embed: The Role of Social Context in Decision Making,* was published on August 3, 2006. Mauboussin's new book, *More Than You Know,* includes much of the material from the *Consilient Observer* series.

Acknowledgments

This book reflects some of what I learned in a decade on Wall Street and in the five years since. I am grateful to all those who shared their time and thoughts, including many whose names do not appear here.

Kenneth French, finance professor at Dartmouth and co-author of some the most important investment research of the last two decades, patiently explained why much of what I learned on Wall Street was irrelevant. Amor Towles of Select Equity and Eunice Panetta of Kaintuck Capital took time to share thoughts on a draft and bolster my faith in the wisdom of (some) active investors. Mark Hebner of Index Funds Advisors shared passion and the extraordinary resources assembled on IFA.com.

Kimbrough Towles and Jeff Jacobs provided thoughts about financial advisors. Ezra Mager and Amos Hostetter offered a real-world perspective on hedge fund selection. Virginia Syer, Ed McCabe, Steve Balog and Chris Kotowski contributed insights about investment research. Andrew Smithers, Richard Bernstein and Michael Mauboussin shared their thoughts and work, which is some of the most original and valuable research on Wall Street. Directly and indirectly, David Swensen, John Bogle, Charles Ellis, Jeremy Grantham, David Siminoff and others taught me most of what I know about intelligent investing.

Purdue professor Leigh Raymond provided his usual blend of encouragement and counsel on an early draft, as did Scott Zumwalt and Sebastian Heath. John Zilliax, Elizabeth Bogner, and Amy Zilliax performed emergency structural surgery. My father, the original Henry Blodget, described some of the bad advice he has heard over the years, including septuagenarians urged to dump stocks for distressed Worldcom bonds and gold. Morris Miller and Dan Horan reminded me what it is like to do business with Wall Street without having spent ten years working there.

Andrew Wylie, Jeff Posternak and Kate Prentice at the Wylie Agency responded instantly and with their customary wisdom and diligence. Jim Atlas and Jessica Fjeld of Atlas Books championed the idea and then made the text readable. Jacob Weisberg, David Plotz and Cliff Sloan of *Slate* welcomed me aboard when doing so was unpopular, as did Andy Bowers of NPR, Joe Nocera at *Fortune* and others. Jacob, David and the *Slate* copy team also expertly edited the original series.

Despite all this expert help, the book no doubt still contains mistakes. I alone am responsible for them.